REDISCOVER LENT

MATTHEW KELLY

REDISCOVER LENT

ST. ANTHONY MESSENGER PRESS
Cincinnati, Ohio

Excerpts from *Rediscover Catholicism: A Spiritual Guide to Living with Passion & Purpose* (Cincinnati: Beacon Publishing, 2011) used by permission of Beacon Publishing. All rights reserved. Scripture passages have been taken from *New Revised Standard Version Bible*, copyright ©1989 by the Division of Christian Education of the National Council of the Churches of Christ in the U.S.A., and used by permission. All rights reserved.

Cover and book design by Mark Sullivan
Cover image © istockphoto | helenecanada

LIBRARY OF CONGRESS CATALOGING-IN-PUBLICATION DATA
Kelly, Matthew.
Rediscover Lent / Matthew Kelly.
p. cm.
Includes bibliographical references and index.
ISBN 978-1-61636-237-9 (alk. paper)
1. Lent—Prayers and devotions. 2. Catholic Church—Prayers and devotions. I. Title.
BX2170.L4K45 2012
242'.34--dc23

2011036646

ISBN 978-1-61636-237-9

Copyright ©2011, Matthew Kelly. All rights reserved.

Published by St. Anthony Messenger Press
28 W. Liberty St.
Cincinnati, OH 45202
www.AmericanCatholic.org
www.SAMPBooks.org

Printed in the United States of America.
Printed on acid-free paper.

12 13 14 15 16   5 4 3 2 1

CONTENTS

THE FOURTH PILLAR: THE BIBLE

THE FIFTH PILLAR: FASTING

THE SIXTH PILLAR: SPIRITUAL READING

INTRODUCTION

The people of every age yearn for God. We have a longing to draw nearer to and a desire to be in communion with God.

My favorite passage from the *Catechism of the Catholic Church* (*CCC*) appears as the first line of the first chapter, and it reads, "The desire for God is written in the human heart, because man is created by God and for God; and God never ceases to draw man to himself. Only in God will he find the truth and happiness he never stops searching for" (*CCC* #1).

One of the greatest tragedies of modern Catholicism is that as Catholics we are no longer considered a spiritual people. If you polled people on the streets of any city in America today and asked them to list five words to describe Catholics, I suspect only a small percentage would say "prayerful" or "spiritual." The tragedy, however, is not how people perceive Catholics, but the possibility that the perception may reflect the reality. It is a generalization, but as Catholics in this modern climate, we tend not to take our spirituality seriously.

Over the coming weeks of Lent, I invite you to reflect with me on the seven pillars of Catholic spirituality. These anchors of our faith combine two thousand years of spiritual wisdom into a handful of spiritual exercises. They may be ancient practices, but don't let that fool you into believing that they are not relevant to your life in the modern world. These practices are dynamic and ever fresh.

Every now and then we read about natural disasters like tsunamis or hurricanes that devastate cities with enormous waves. Watching the television footage, I am always amazed that some trees are able to withstand the wind and waves while everything else is blown away. *How do they do it?*

With strong, deep roots.

A tree with deep roots can weather any storm. In your life and mine it is only a matter of time before the next storm gets here: an illness, the death of a loved one, unemployment, financial difficulties, a troubled child, a natural disaster, marital strife, or any number of other things. The storms of life are inevitable.

And so the question is not whether there will be another storm. The question is: When will the next storm get here? And when the next storm gets here, it's too late to sink the roots. When the next storm gets here, you either have the roots or you don't.

Sink these roots, the seven pillars of Catholic spirituality, deep into your life and you will weather any storm. But more than that, so much more than surviving the storms of life, you will come to know the abundant life that Jesus invites us to experience both here and in eternity.

HOW TO USE THIS BOOK

. . . .

This book is an attempt to raise morale among Catholics, to remind ourselves that there is genius in Catholicism, and to engage disengaged Catholics in a particular way during the lenten season. It uses the lectionary readings for Lent as a backdrop for the reflections, which were taken from the book *Rediscover Catholicism*.

Each day, I encourage you to read the Scripture selections for the day, then the reflection that follows. Next, spend some time in meditation on the Scripture and on the reflection. Finally, there is an opportunity for prayer.

My hope is that in the process of going more deeply into our faith this Lent, we will draw closer to God and find a richer expression of our faith. As well, we will explore what it means to be Catholic in this place and in this time.

Our spiritual heritage is rich in wisdom and practice. If we can embrace this heritage and adapt it to the modern context, we will begin again to thrive as the spiritual people God intended us to be—both individually and as a Church.

THE FIRST PILLAR: CONFESSION

. . . .

Ash Wednesday

JOEL 2:12–18; 2 CORINTHIANS 5:20—6:2; MATTHEW 6:1–6, 16–18

BE RECONCILED TO GOD

. . . .

So we are ambassadors for Christ, since God is making his appeal
through us; we entreat you on behalf of Christ, be reconciled to
God…. For he says, "At an acceptable time I have listened to you,
and on a day of salvation I have helped you." See, now is the
acceptable time; see, now is the day of salvation!

(2 Corinthians 5:20, 6:2)

. . . .

REFLECTION

I have spent much of my adult life speaking to groups around the
world about the seven pillars of Catholic spirituality. One of the
questions I am asked most often is, "Why do you put confession

first?" Others will say, "You should let people warm up and get comfortable before you drop confession on them." But there is a reason I placed Confession as the first of the seven pillars.

When John the Baptist first appeared in the desert of Judea, this was his message: "Repent, prepare the way of the Lord" (Matthew 3:2). Later, when Jesus began his ministry, he led with this message: "Repent, for the kingdom of heaven is at hand" (Matthew 4:17).

Repent is a powerful word. But what does it mean for you and me, here and now, more than two thousand years later? It means the same as it did to the people walking around the dusty pathways in their sandals, trying to inch closer to Jesus as he passed through their town or village. Repent means "to turn back to God."

I find myself needing to turn back to God many times a day, in ways small and large. It is not a matter of guilt and it is not a shameful thing. It is simply that at his side I am a better person—a better son, husband, father, brother, friend, employer, and citizen. Over time, I have also come to realize, quite painfully, that when I turn away from God I am also turning my back on my true self.

MEDITATION

Where do I stand in my relationship with God? Do I need to turn back to God today?

PRAYER

God of goodness and mercy, hear my prayer this lenten season. Let me be honest with myself as I look into my heart and soul, noticing the times I turn away from you, then seeking to repent and return to your love. May humility guide my efforts to be reconciled with you and live forever in your abundant grace. Amen.

Thursday After Ash Wednesday

DEUTERONOMY 30:15–20; LUKE 9:22–25

IMPERFECT BUT PERFECTIBLE

. . . .

What does it profit them if they gain the whole world,

but lose or forfeit themselves?

(Luke 9:25)

. . . .

REFLECTION

Every journey toward something is a journey away from something. If we need to turn back to God at this moment in our lives, we also need to turn away from whatever led us away from God and keeps us away. It may be that certain people have led you to stray from God—perhaps possessions have distracted you from your true and authentic self, or maybe pleasure has seduced you into walking a wayward path.

Whatever has distracted you, it is important to realize that you cannot journey to a new place and at the same time stay where you are. Walking with God demands that we bring order to our lives and put first things first. Sometimes it is just as important to know what you are journeying away from as it is to know what you are journeying toward.

The journey toward the-best-version-of-yourself is a journey away from the defects of the-present-version-of-yourself. Every day I find myself doing things that are self-destructive and that make me a lesser person. I say things that hurt others, or I hurt others by not saying things. These are the thoughts, words, and actions that deviate from the natural order and separate me from the peace of knowing I am contributing positively to the common good of the unfolding universe. I find myself experiencing what Paul described: "The good that I would I do not, and the evil that I would not it is that which I do" (Romans 7:19).

We are all imperfect but perfectible. The Church holds us in our weakness, comforts us in our limitations, endeavors to heal us of our sickness, and nurtures us back to health, making us whole again. And throughout this process, the Church manages to harness all our efforts and struggles, not only for our own good but for the good of the entire Church—indeed, for all humanity.

MEDITATION

Can I honestly examine the sins and shortcomings that keep me from being the-best-version-of-myself? Am I willing to be more attentive to what God is calling me to be?

PRAYER

God of humility and truth, hear my prayer this lenten season. Point me toward the path that leads to you. Help me to get to know myself better, so that I may know how to improve and ultimately become the-best-version-of-myself for you. Amen.

Friday After Ash Wednesday

ISAIAH 58:1–9A; MATTHEW 9:14–15

THE JOY OF A CLEAR CONSCIENCE

. . . .

Is not this the fast that I choose:

to loose the bonds of injustice,

to undo the thongs of the yoke,

to let the oppressed go free,

and to break every yoke?

(Isaiah 58:6)

. . . .

REFLECTION

We all do things every day that are contrary to the ways of God, things that stop us from being the-best-version-of-ourselves. Then we carry all this baggage around with us and it affects us in ways that we are often not even aware of. Our sins affect us physically, emotionally, intellectually, spiritually, and psychologically. They affect our

7

relationships, our work, our health, our intellectual clarity, and our ability to genuinely embrace and experience all of life.

Sin limits our future by chaining us to the past. Yet, most people are able to convince themselves either that sin doesn't exist, that they don't sin, or that their sins are not affecting them. But if we take an honest inventory of our thoughts, words, and actions, it becomes abundantly clear that every one of us does things that are self-destructive, offensive to others, contrary to the natural laws of the universe, and in direct conflict with the ways of God. If we really think that we can carry all this around inside us and that it is not affecting us, then we are only deceiving ourselves.

If you want peace in your heart, I want to personally invite you to go to confession. There is no treasure in life like a clear conscience. If you want the joy of a clear conscience, go to confession. If you haven't been to confession for a while, maybe now is your time. Perhaps it has been ten years, or twenty years, maybe even longer. Jesus says to you, "Do not be afraid" (Matthew 14:27). Bring the sins of your life and place them at the feet of Jesus in this sacrament of reconciliation.

God sees your unrealized potential. He sees not only who you are but also who you can be. Ask him to share that vision with you.

MEDITATION

Am I willing to make confession a regular part of my life? How and when will I begin?

PRAYER

God of compassion and forgiveness, hear my prayer this lenten season. Grant me your grace and healing. Give me the strength to be honest about my own shortcomings and sins. Help me to renew my resolve to be a better person and start anew. Amen.

Saturday After Ash Wednesday

Isaiah 58:9b–14; Luke 5:27–32

GET TO KNOW YOURSELF

. . . .

Jesus answered, "Those who are well have no need of a physician, but those who are sick; I have come to call not the righteous but sinners to repentance."

(Luke 5:31–32)

. . . .

REFLECTION

In the spiritual life, it is very important to grow not only in our knowledge and understanding of God but also in knowledge and understanding of ourselves. Confessing our sins in the sacrament of reconciliation helps us to develop this self-knowledge. The saints hungered for it. They developed it from hours of self-examination and consistent practice of confession.

The saints knew their strengths and weaknesses, their faults, failings, and flaws, their talents and abilities, their needs and desires, their hopes and dreams, their potential and their purpose. They were not afraid to look at themselves as they really were by the light of God's grace in prayer. They knew that the things of this world are passing and that, when this brief life is over, we will each stand naked in the presence of God. At that moment, money, power, status, possessions, and worldly fame will mean nothing. The only thing that has value in that moment is character—the light within you. As Francis of Assisi once said, "Remember, you are what you are in the eyes of God, and nothing else."

Get to know yourself. The gifts of self-knowledge include freedom from the world's image of who you are (and who you should be) and an unquenchable compassion for others. The more I get to know myself (and my own brokenness), the more I am able to accept and love others. Furthermore, the more I get to know myself and my sinfulness, the more I am able to understand others and tolerate their faults, failings, flaws, addictions, and brokenness. Self-knowledge breeds the ultimate form of compassion.

Self-knowledge also deflates all the false pride and egotism in our lives. Genuine self-knowledge is humbling, and two humble people will always have a better relationship than two prideful people. Not sometimes. Always.

MEDITATION

How well do I know myself? Is there someone I can talk to this Lent who can help me to assess both my talents and my failings?

PRAYER

All-knowing and compassionate God, hear my prayer this lenten season. Help me to accept all that I am and all that you have created me to be. Help me to recognize my own sinful ways that are keeping me from becoming my most authentic and true self. Help me to see the authentic beauty and integrity you have created in others too, so that I may judge them less and accept them more. Amen.

THE SECOND PILLAR: DAILY PRAYER

· ·

Sunday of the First Week of Lent

YEAR A: GENESIS 2:7–9, 3:1–7; ROMANS 5:12–19; MATTHEW 4:1–11

YEAR B: GENESIS 9:8–15; 1 PETER 3:18–22; MARK 1:12–15

YEAR C: DEUTERONOMY 26:4–10; ROMANS 10:8–13; LUKE 4:1–13

PRAYER IS AN EVERYDAY THING

· ·

Jesus said to him, "Away with you, Satan! for it is written,

'Worship the Lord your God,

and serve only him.'"

(Matthew 4:10)

· ·

REFLECTION

Prayer is central to the Christian experience. A Christian life is not sustainable without it, because growth in the Christian life is simply not possible without prayer. Growing in character and virtue, learning to hear the voice of God in our lives and walking where he calls us—all require the discipline of prayer. And it is not enough simply to pray when we feel like it. Prayer requires a daily commitment.

Many people fail to establish a daily habit of prayer in their lives because they approach it with the wrong expectations. Consciously or subconsciously, most people approach prayer expecting it to be easy. The truth is, prayer is perhaps the most difficult thing we will ever do. From time to time, we may get carried away by a moment of inspiration in our prayer, but for the most part prayer is hard work—work well worth doing, but hard work nonetheless.

You don't become a great athlete by training only when you feel like it. You don't become a great writer by writing only when you feel inspired to write. And the saints did not become such fine ambassadors of God on earth by praying only when they felt like praying. In each case, a daily discipline is required.

If you neglect prayer for a day, you are probably the only person who can tell. But you can tell. You have less patience and you are less focused. If you neglect prayer for a week, several people around you will notice the change in you. But if you neglect prayer for two or three weeks, almost everyone around you will recognize that you are not at your best.

It is has been almost twenty years now since I began a serious habit of prayer in my life. Now I cannot imagine a life without prayer. I don't know how people survive in our crazy, noisy, busy world without the sanctuary of prayer to renew and refresh them. There are many reasons to pray and many ways to pray—what is critical is that we make an effort to create a daily habit of prayer in our lives.

MEDITATION

What are my prayer habits? Do I take time each day to speak with God?

PRAYER

Loving God, guide my every move that I may act in your name and by your will. Let me be attentive to your word and listen for your voice within the deepest reaches of my heart. May my prayer rise like incense in thanksgiving and praise. Amen.

Monday of the First Week of Lent

LEVITICUS 19:1–2, 11–18; MATTHEW 25:31–46

WHY DO YOU PRAY?

. . . .

And the king will answer them, "Truly I tell you, just as you did it

to one of the least of these who are members of my family,

you did it to me."

(Matthew 25:40)

. . . .

REFLECTION

A while ago I was visiting a grade school, and a child, perhaps seven years old, asked me, "Why do you pray?" Dozens of thoughts flashed through my mind, all of which may have suited an adult or a theologian, but I couldn't find the words to express them to a child. So, I asked him a question instead of answering his. I asked him the same question he had asked me: "Why do you pray?"

He didn't have to think about it. Spontaneously and casually he said, "Well, God is my friend, and friends like to know what is going on in each other's lives."

Sometimes I pray for very selfish reasons. Perhaps I am stressed and overwhelmed, and I go to prayer hoping God will calm my heart and mind and bring peace to my soul. Sometimes I pray for completely altruistic reasons. When some region of the world is torn apart by natural disaster or war, I often find myself driven to prayer. Sometimes I pray for very holy reasons. There are times when I pray not because I want something from God but just to express my gratitude for all the things, people, and opportunities he has filled my life with. And when I am at my best, I pray simply to be with God and seek his ways.

Most of the time I pray for more practical reasons—three in particular. First, I pray to make sense of things. I also pray because I want to live life deeply and deliberately. Finally, I pray to build up the kind of inner density required to prevent the culture from swallowing me up. If we are going to be true to our values, if we are going to celebrate and defend the-best-version-of-ourselves, we need to build up a certain density within us. This inner strength, or density, will allow us to resist the cultural pressure to abandon our values, our true selves, and God.

MEDITATION

Why do I pray? Do I need to rethink the reasons I am praying and refocus my intentions?

PRAYER

Listening and patient God, I come to you every day as my trusted friend. Know that I am your friend too, and I am here to do your will. Let your voice fill my heart with gratitude, patience, strength, and peace. Amen.

Tuesday of the First Week of Lent

Isaiah 55:10–11; Matthew 6:7–15

YOU ARE WHAT YOU THINK

. . . .

For as the rain and the snow come down from heaven,

and do not return there until they have watered the earth,

making it bring forth and sprout,

giving seed to the sower and bread to the eater,

so shall my word be that goes out from my mouth.

(Isaiah 55:10–11)

. . . .

REFLECTION

The difference between the saints and those who have been less successful in living the Christian life is that the saints affixed their singleness of purpose on doing the will of God. They also had better habits than many of us—not only external habits but also internal habits. One of those critical internal habits is the habit of the mind we call contemplation.

Contemplation is not just for saints, monks, and nuns. In truth, we all lead lives of contemplation, but we spend our lives contemplating very different things. What do you contemplate? Is it the riches of the world? Is it every man or woman who passes you in the street? Do you ponder the latest fashions? The local gossip? Or do you contemplate the wonders of God, the glory of his creation, and the joys of the spiritual life?

Prayer and contemplation are integral to the Christian life because thought determines action. If you send your thoughts down one road, your actions will follow your thoughts. Thought determines action, and so the actions of your life are determined by your most dominant thoughts.

As you move from one activity to the next in your day, become aware of what you are thinking and how different thoughts make you feel. Become aware of the thoughts that encourage you to love God and those around you more, and those thoughts that don't. Then consciously try to focus more and more of your thinking on those that do.

It is not necessary to go away to a monastery to live a life of contemplation. We are all contemplatives because we are all thinking all the time, and what you contemplate will play a very significant role in the life you live.

MEDITATION

What most occupies my thoughts throughout the day? Is God usually at the center of my mind, or am I more often distracted by the things of this world?

PRAYER

Steadfast and loyal, God, you are always thinking of me and all of your creation. Help me to think of you more and of trivial and temporal things less. Guide me to contemplate what will nourish and enrich my soul—and the lives of all those I touch. Amen.

COME INTO THE SILENCE

· ·

The people of Nineveh will rise up at the judgment with this gener-
ation and condemn it, because they repented at the proclamation of
Jonah, and see, something greater than Jonah is here!

(Luke 11:32)

· ·

REFLECTION

I am convinced that in this modern time it is not that God has
stopped speaking to us but rather that we have stopped listening.
And while I believe that God can communicate through anyone and
anything at any time, his preferred venue is still silence and solitude.
In the silence God speaks. Or perhaps it is just that in the silence,
away from the hustle and bustle of the world, we are able to hear
him.

22

In the silence you will find God and in the silence you will find yourself. In the silence things start to make sense. Consider this example: You are taking a road trip with friends and you get lost and a little turned around. You feel confused. What do you do? Do you tell the people you are traveling with to talk louder and turn the music up? No. You ask everyone to be quiet and you turn the music off. Why?

Things start to make sense in the silence.

It can be very hard to find a quiet place in this world. How do you imagine that in the midst of all that noise you are going to work out who you are and what you are here for? Unless you withdraw from all the noise of your life and the world for a few minutes each day, you will most likely just become another cog in the global economic wheel, consuming and being consumed.

Quietness is essential to the growth in the Spirit. Your soul needs silence like you need air to breathe and water to drink. While the modern world is filling up with more and more noise, God is inviting us into the silence and into his presence. Here, in the presence of

God, we will find rest for our weary hearts and minds. In the great classroom of silence we will develop resolute hearts and peaceful spirits.

MEDITATION

Find some time today to be silent for at least ten minutes. Open your heart and listen to what God is saying to you, right here, right now.

PRAYER

God of silence and peace, help me to be more like you. Allow me to listen more closely and attentively to all that you are calling me to do and be. Show me how to be still in the chaos and bustle of the world. My weary heart and mind long for rest and peace in you. Amen.

Thursday of the First Week of Lent

Esther C: 12, 14–16, 23–25; Matthew 7:7–12

WHAT SHOULD I DO?

. . . .

Ask, and it will be given you; search, and you will find; knock, and

the door will be opened for you. For everyone who asks receives,

and everyone who searches finds, and for everyone who knocks,

the door will be opened.

(Matthew 7:7–8)

. . . .

REFLECTION

Our lives change when our habits change. My life changed when, encouraged by a friend, I began to pray for ten minutes a day. In those quiet moments of reflection I stumbled upon the big question: *God, what do you think I should do?*

Ignatius asked the question. Francis asked the question. Benedict asked the question. Dominic asked the question. Joan of Arc asked the question. Theresa asked the question. Will you? These men and women began by asking a very simple question: *God, what do you think I should do?* And as a result of constantly asking this question they became spiritual giants.

When was the last time you sat down with the Divine Architect and asked, God, what do you think I should do in this situation with my spouse? When was the last time you asked, God, what do you think I should do in this situation at work? When your kids come to you to talk about what they are thinking of doing with their lives, do you just ask them what they want to do? Or do you ask them what they feel God is calling them to do?

Henry David Thoreau said, "Most men lead lives of quiet desperation." If you don't ask the big question, you won't discover your mission, and sooner or later you will be numbered among Thoreau's masses. You won't plan to live a life of quiet desperation; nobody does. You'll just wake up one morning and realize you already are living one—and wonder how it happened.

If you are already living a life of quiet desperation, you don't have to stay there. Just start asking the big question. *God, what do you think I should do?* In the moments of the day ask the question. In your daily prayer, ask the question. Make this one question a constant part of your inner dialogue, and I promise you, your life will start to change.

MEDITATION

God, what do you think I should do? Am I living the life you have called me to?

PRAYER

All-knowing and understanding God, help me discern what habits I need to change or get rid of altogether. Help me to replace negative and self-destructive habits with positive ones that will improve my life and lead me closer to you. Help me to know what it is that you want me to do. Amen.

MAKE TIME TO PRAY

. . . .

If you remember that your brother or sister has something against you, leave your gift there at the altar and go; first be reconciled to your brother or sister and then come and offer your gift.

(Matthew 5:23–24)

. . . .

REFLECTION

Perhaps you are concerned that you don't know how to pray. It is much simpler than you suppose. Step into the silence and, in your heart, say to God, "I don't know how to pray," and already you will have begun to pray. Just talk to him. Simply open your heart to him in a gentle dialogue. Speak to him as you would a great friend, mentor, coach, or teacher.

When you leave your time of prayer, continue the dialogue with God in your heart throughout the moments of your day. Share with him your joys and your disappointments, your questions and your doubts. Speak to him about everything.

Tevye, from the musical *Fiddler on the Roof*, is a great example. He is always talking to God, about everything. This constant dialogue is perhaps part of what Paul had in mind when he wrote, "Pray constantly" (1 Thessalonians 5:17).

Begin with ten minutes. In time you may feel called to spend more time. If that is the case, I encourage you to increase the time you spend in prayer gradually and consistently. I would also encourage you to keep track of what days you do it, what days you don't, and how long you spend in prayer each day.

In my work as a business consultant, one of the greatest lessons I have learned is that the best companies measure everything. They have a fundamental understanding that if you don't measure it you won't change it. As a result I started measuring how much time I spent in prayer each day. I wrote it down on a piece of paper throughout the day, and at the end of each week I tallied it up. I was surprised to see how little time I spent in prayer.

I would like to encourage you to measure how much time you spend in prayer each week. You will be amazed how measuring this time allows you to focus and grow in your prayer life.

MEDITATION

How much time will I devote to prayer today? In what ways must my life change to make prayer a regular part of my life?

PRAYER

Constant and unchanging God, show me how to be more like you. Help me to come to rely on you for everything and pray to you without ceasing—today and always. Amen.

Saturday of the First Week of Lent

DEUTERONOMY 26:16–19; MATTHEW 5:43–48

PRAYER LEADS TO DEEP PLACES

. . . .

Love your enemies and pray for those who persecute you, so that
you may be children of your Father in heaven; for he makes his
sun rise on the evil and on the good, and sends rain on the
righteous and on the unrighteous.

(Matthew 5:45–46)

. . . .

REFLECTION

When my soul is hungry I often think of the passage in Luke's Gospel
where Simon and his friends have been fishing all night without
catching anything. Jesus says to him, "Put out into the deep water
and lower your nets for a catch" (Luke 5:4).

You can imagine what Simon is thinking to himself. He has been
fishing all night and this is his profession and he has caught nothing,
and now Jesus, who has no knowledge or experience of fishing, is

telling him to get back out there and lower his nets. If they were fishing all night you can be sure they are tired. If they caught nothing you can be sure they are frustrated. And it is important to note that putting out into the deep water and lowering the nets is not a five- or ten-minute exercise. Jesus is making a significant request.

Perhaps at this time in your life you are tired and frustrated—with your career, with your marriage, with your children, with society, with your spiritual life—but Jesus is saying to you, "Put out into the deep water and lower your nets for a catch."

In the story we know that Simon and his friends listen to Jesus and do what he suggests, and they catch so many fish that their nets begin to tear and they need help from fishermen in other boats to haul in the catch.

Over and over in life, God challenges us to abandon our doubts and fears and cast our nets into the deep waters of the spiritual life. It is never convenient, it is almost always difficult, and it is some- times quite painful, but if we heed the Lord's direction we will always bring in a huge catch. Don't be afraid of the deep places.

MEDITATION

Where are the deep places in my life right now? What is God calling
me to do here?

PRAYER

God of deep waters and infinite riches, challenge me to go where I
fear, to do what is difficult and what I thought could never be done.
Push me to go to the deep waters of life and cast my net wide, for I
put all my hope, trust, and faith in you. Amen.

THE THIRD PILLAR: THE MASS

Sunday of the Second Week of Lent

YEAR A: GENESIS 12:1–4; 2 TIMOTHY 1:8–10; MATTHEW 17:1–9

YEAR B: GENESIS 22:1–2, 9, 10–13, 15–18; ROMANS 8:31–34; MARK 9:2–10

YEAR C: GENESIS 15:5–12, 17–18; PHILIPPIANS 3:17—4:1; LUKE 9:28–36

MASS IS NOT BORING

While he was still speaking, suddenly a bright cloud overshadowed them, and from the cloud a voice said, "This is my Son, the Beloved; with him I am well pleased; listen to him!"

(Matthew 17:5)

REFLECTION

The Mass is at the center of Catholic tradition, and yet the general consensus today seems to be that Mass is boring. We have become used to hearing children say, "I don't want to go to church. Mass is boring!" Worse yet, more and more adults are saying, "Mass is boring!" "It's not relevant to my modern life!"

Some people say the problem with the Mass is the way the altar servers behave, others say the problem is that the music is too modern or too old-fashioned, while still others say that the problem with the Mass is the readers, the eucharistic ministers, the parking lot, the coffee they serve after Mass, or their priest's homilies. We have tried to make Mass more engaging by changing things, adding things, and involving more and more people, but despite all of this, an increasing number of people have stopped attending Mass on a regular basis and profess to be bored or actively disengaged during Mass.

In truth, there is no problem with the Mass. People of all places and times have found it to be the life-transforming centerpiece of their spiritual lives. Many people, young and old, still find Mass to be an experience that provides incredibly spiritual comfort and clarity.

I am not willing to accept that Mass is irrelevant to our lives, though I do think we need to consider if our lives are irrelevant to

Mass. I am willing to accept that many, many people are bored at Mass; they have no reason to lie. The question is, how do we move them beyond their boredom to a richer experience of the Mass? How do we demonstrate the powerful relevance of the Mass?

There are more than a billion Catholics on the planet. The central experience of Catholicism is the Mass, and I believe that we have an obligation together as a Church to engage people.

MEDITATION

Do I find Mass to be an integral part of my faith life? Or am I simply going through the motions?

PRAYER

Almighty Father, each time we attend Mass we remember the sacrifice made by your son, Jesus, who died that we might be saved. May I cherish the chance to worship you each week at Sunday liturgy, and encourage others to love and understand this powerful prayer of the Church. Amen.

HEAR THE WORD OF THE LORD

. . . .

We have sinned and done wrong, acted wickedly and rebelled, turning aside from your commandments and ordinances. We have not listened to your servants the prophets, who spoke in your name to our kings, our princes, and our ancestors, and to all the people of the land.

(Daniel 9:5–6)

. . . .

REFLECTION

I believe the Word of God has the power to transform our lives. I have experienced this power in my own life and witnessed it in the lives of countless others. The Word of God can have a powerful impact in your life too, beginning today.

But the Word of God will not transform your life, or mine, with one quick reading on a Sunday morning in a church full of people, where we are surrounded by a thousand distractions. In order to deliver its soothing waters to our souls, the Word of God needs an opportunity to linger in our minds and to sink its roots deep into our hearts. And it's very difficult for this to take place in the context of Sunday Mass.

The priest stands up to read the Gospel and everyone in church rises to their feet. At that moment, you get distracted by who is at church or who is not at church, by what someone is wearing or what someone is not wearing, by a child running up and down the aisle throwing his crayons and eating a snack, or throwing his snack and eating his crayons. The next thing you know, the priest is beginning his homily. You have no idea what the Gospel was about and you go home spiritually undernourished.

What was last Sunday's Gospel reading? Maybe you know and maybe you don't. My experience has been that more than 90 percent of Catholics can't tell you what last Sunday's Gospel was about. If we don't know what last Sunday's Gospel reading was, only a few days later, then I have to believe that it didn't significantly impact our lives.

MEDITATION

What impact does the Word of God have on me as I attend Sunday Mass? Do I allow the readings to penetrate into my heart and soul, or am I usually oblivious to what is going on?

PRAYER

God the Father who sent us your son, Jesus, at each Mass let me ponder this ultimate sacrifice and your love for all your children of creation. May I actively engage in the Scripture readings and listen more attentively to the homily, so that my life can be enriched and renewed in you each week. Amen.

Tuesday of the Second Week of Lent

ISAIAH 1:10, 16–20; MATTHEW 23:1–12

MAKE TIME TO PREPARE

· ·

But you are not to be called rabbi, for you have one teacher, and you are all students. And call no one your father on earth, for you have one Father—the one in heaven.

(Matthew 23:8–9)

· ·

REFLECTION

Preparation may be the most powerful tool at your disposal to improve your experience of the Mass. We know the value of preparation in business, at school, and in sports, so why wouldn't the same truth apply when it comes to Mass? Preparation elevates every worthwhile human endeavor.

I would like to suggest that once a week, perhaps on Tuesday or Wednesday, you take time to read and reflect on the coming Sunday's

Gospel. Just start with the Gospel. Perhaps in time you will move on to reflect on all of the readings, but for now, just start with the Gospel. If you are married, you may wish to share this experience with your spouse.

Don't just rush through it. Read next Sunday's Gospel slowly and pick out a word or a phrase that strikes you or jumps out at you. Take turns reading and then explaining which word jumped out at you. Then read through it again. Again, be attentive for a word or phrase that strikes you. Maybe it will be the same word; maybe it will be a different word. It doesn't matter. Read the passage three times. If the Word of God is to transform us we need to allow it to sink its roots deep into our lives through repetition and reflection.

Each time, think about why that particular word or phrase is prodding you. Is there something happening in your life that this word or phrase speaks to? Is there something you should be doing that makes this word or phrase prick your conscience? Perhaps there is something you shouldn't be doing, and this word convicts you. Or maybe a word comforts or inspires you.

When you familiarize yourself with next Sunday's Gospel, the Mass will no longer be just part of your routine. It will become a spiritual experience and part of your own personal adventure of salvation.

MEDITATION

Can I take time this week to read the Gospel for next Sunday? Am I willing to commit this Lent to letting God's Word sink deeply into my life?

PRAYER

My One True Father, help me to think of you more often in my daily life. May I rely on you as I would my own father for advice, encouragement, and solace. May I come to you prepared each week—knowing what you expect from me and what is mine to do in your name. Amen.

SHOW ME THE WAY!

. . . .

Jesus answered, "You do not know what you are asking. Are you able to drink the cup that I am about to drink?" They said to him,

"We are able."

(Matthew 20:22)

. . . .

REFLECTION

Having prepared ourselves for Mass, the next step to fully participating in the liturgy is to be at Mass with an open heart and open mind, expecting God to communicate with us. With that in mind I would like to propose a simple approach that could change the whole way we experience the Mass.

When you walk into Mass next Sunday, simply ask God in the quiet of your heart, "God, show me one way in this Mass that I can become a-better-version-of-myself this week!" Then listen. Listen to

43

what God is saying to you in the music, the readings, and the homily. Listen to the prayers of the Mass, and listen to the quiet of your heart. The one way will strike you. Once it is revealed to you, spend the rest of the Mass holding that one way prayerfully in your heart.

We don't go to Mass to socialize. We don't go to be entertained. We go to give ourselves to God, and in return to receive God. Open your heart, open your mind, and open your soul to the miracles God wants to work in and through you.

Mass is not about whom you sit next to. It's not about which priest says Mass. It is not about what you wear or who is there. Mass is not about the music. It's not even about the preaching. It's about gathering as a community to give thanks to God for all the blessings he fills our lives with. It is about receiving the body and blood of Christ, not just physically, but spiritually.

This week, as you prepare yourself to celebrate the Mass on Sunday, be conscious of the marvel, the wonder, the mystery of the Mass. Open your heart and mind to hearing what God offers you this day—your one way.

MEDITATION

What area in my life needs special attention right now? Can I ask God to show me the way to attend to that area this Lent?

PRAYER

Ever-present and Marvelous Father, help me to open my heart, mind, and soul to you. Let me walk into your home prepared to greet, meet, and get to know you better, so that I may become a-better-version-of-myself. Help me to tune out the distractions, so that I may fully participate in the marvelous and wondrous mystery that is the Mass. Amen.

Thursday of the Second Week of Lent

JEREMIAH 17:5–10; LUKE 16:19–31

THE MASS PRAYERS

. . . .

The heart is devious above all else;

it is perverse—

who can understand it?

I the LORD test the mind

and search the heart,

to give to all according to their ways,

according to the fruit of their doings.

(Jeremiah 17:9–10)

. . . .

REFLECTION

There is genius and beauty in the prayers of the Mass, and yet, most people tune out the prayers. It seems to me that keeping God's dream for us to become the-best-version-of-ourselves in the forefront of our mind unlocks the language of the many prayers that make up the Mass.

The prayers of the Mass remind us that we are pilgrims on a journey, that we are not on this journey alone, and that we are called to be responsible stewards of our own lives while at the same time living in a way that is mindful of the needs of others and mindful of the needs of all of creation. Over and over again, the prayers of the Mass orient us toward God and remind us of his desire to have a relationship with us.

There is great beauty in these prayers, but too often we don't hear them because we are distracted by our thoughts or by those around us. Some of the prayers are the same for every Mass. Others change with the seasons of the Church calendar. And still others change every day. If you take time to listen and truly pray these prayers as the priest says them, you will discover the intimate knowledge the Church has of our spiritual needs.

The prayers of the Mass are beautifully integrated and carefully designed to keep us focused on God's dream for us to become the-best-version-of-ourselves. For example, the opening prayers of the Mass guide us to focus on the themes that will emerge in the readings that day. This is the opening prayer for the Thursday after Ash Wednesday: "Lord, may everything we do begin with your inspiration, continue with your help, and reach perfection under your guidance."

The Mass reveals God's vision for us as individuals, his vision for marriage and family, for community and society, and for the Church and the world.

MEDITATION

How well do I know the prayers of the Mass? Have I paid attention to the changes in the prayers that began last Advent?

PRAYER

God of beauty and inspiration, may I listen more intently to your prayers you have given me so that everything I do begins with your inspiration, continues with your help, and reaches perfection under your guidance. Amen.

DELIVER US FROM EVERY EVIL

· ·

Jesus said to them, "Have you never read in the scriptures:

'The stone that the builders rejected

has become the cornerstone;

this was the Lord's doing,

and it is amazing in our eyes'?

Therefore I tell you, the kingdom of God will be taken away from you and given to a people that produces the fruits of the kingdom."

(Matthew 21:42–43)

· ·

REFLECTION

Do you have a favorite prayer in the Mass? Mine is right before the sign of peace, when the priest prays, "Deliver us, Lord, from every evil and grant us peace in our days. In your mercy keep us free from sin, and protect us from all anxiety as we wait in joyful hope for the coming of our Savior, Jesus Christ." These words mean so much to me. To live a life free from sin is a humble and simple ambition, but a noble one.

I have seen how sin complicates our lives, confuses our minds, and hardens our hearts. I have seen the devastating effects of sin in my own life, in the lives of the people I love, and in the lives of complete strangers. I want to live a life free from sin, and the prayer to keep us free from sin resonates with the deepest desires of my heart. I love the peace that is the fruit of a clear conscience. The truth is, the happiest times of my life have been when I was actively trying to live free from sin.

"Protect us from all anxiety"—all anxiety, not some anxiety. How much of our lives do we waste worrying? A friend of mine has a quote by Corrie ten Boom on her answering machine that says, "Worry doesn't empty tomorrow of its suffering; it empties today of its strength."

I know it is the sin in my life that causes my pain, anguish, impatience, anxiety, irritableness, restlessness, and discontentment. We waste so much time and energy on sin. Imagine how much you and I could accomplish if we didn't waste so much time and energy on sin!

MEDITATION

Do I have a favorite prayer in the Mass? What is it about this prayer that resonates with me?

PRAYER

God of peace and serenity, protect me from all anxiety. Guide me to make good choices, so that I may not sin and cause myself or others needless worry and anxiety as "I wait in joyful hope for the coming of our Savior, Jesus Christ." Amen.

THE MASS UNITES US

. . . .

Who is a God like you, pardoning iniquity

and passing over the transgression

of the remnant of your possession?

He does not retain his anger forever,

because he delights in showing clemency.

(Micah 7:18)

. . . .

REFLECTION

At every moment of every day the Mass is being celebrated all over the world. In the Mass, the more than 1.1 billion Catholics around the world come together to share a common experience. Through the Mass, we pray as Catholics not only for ourselves and our own needs but for the whole human family.

The wisdom of regular worship has a much deeper meaning than bringing us all together once a week; it is a profound reflection of God's blueprint for all of creation. Rhythm is at the core of God's genius for creation, and we are invited to use this same blueprint for our life. The seasons change to a rhythm. The tides come in and go out to a rhythm. The sun rises and sets to a rhythm. Your heart pumps blood through your body to a rhythm. Rhythm gives birth to harmony, efficiency, effectiveness, health, happiness, peace, and prosperity. Destroy the rhythm and you invite chaos, confusion, destruction, and disorder.

The Church bases the liturgical calendar on the rhythm that God has placed at the center of creation. In turn, the Church hopes this will help us to place this essential rhythm at the center of our own lives. It is within this context that we can begin to understand Sunday as a day of rest and renewal, and more specifically the role of the Mass in the Catholic lifestyle.

God doesn't call us to church because he has some egotistical need for us all to fall down before him and worship him at ten o'clock each

Sunday morning. It isn't designed to help him; it's designed to help us.

There is a beautiful song titled "Come to the Feast Divine," written by Liam Lawton, from his album *In the Quiet*. It begins with a simple question, "Will you come to the Feast Divine?" I hope you will. The Mass is filled with riches. It is an unfathomable gift; embrace it.

MEDITATION

Have I come to a better understanding and appreciation of the Mass during this week? What are a few of the ways my participation in the Mass can become more profound this Lent?

PRAYER

God of rhythm and order, thank you for giving us your divine blessing of rest, renewal, and communion with you and others through the Mass. Thank you for giving me the opportunity each week to restore harmony, efficiency, health, happiness, peace, order, prosperity, hope, and love back to my life. Amen.

THE FOURTH PILLAR: THE BIBLE

Sunday of the Third Week of Lent

YEAR A: EXODUS 17:3–7; ROMANS 5:1–2, 5–8; JOHN 4:5–42

YEAR B: EXODUS 20:1–17; 1 CORINTHIANS 1:22–25; JOHN 2:13–25

YEAR C: EXODUS 3:1–8, 13–15; 1 CORINTHIANS 10:1–6, 10–12; LUKE 13:1–9

WHAT IS THE BIBLE?

Jesus said to her, "Everyone who drinks of this water will be thirsty again, but those who drink of the water that I will give them will never be thirsty. The water that I will give will become in them a spring of water gushing up to eternal life."

(John 4:13–14)

REFLECTION

Of all the books ever written or published, the Bible is the most widely read, studied, translated, printed, sold, gifted, distributed, and quoted. It is the bestselling book of all time. When it comes to teaching about the nature of God and his desires for us, no other book comes close. In the Bible, we discover the depth and generosity of God's love as well as his desire to soothe humanity's yearning for truth and happiness.

Where did the Bible come from? How did we come to be blessed with such a rare treasure? Well, it didn't just drop down from heaven one fine day, nor did it appear suddenly on the earth, delivered by an angel of God. The Bible was written with some form of primitive inks and pens by people just like you and me. They were divinely inspired in a way that none of us will fully understand in this life, but they were ordinary people with strengths and weaknesses.

The Bible isn't a book. It is a collection of books—seventy-three in all: forty-six in the Old Testament and twenty-seven in the New Testament. Hence the name *Biblia* in Greek, which means "the books" or "library." It is important to note that most Protestant and Evangelical Bibles contain only sixty-six books. It was during the

Reformation that non-Catholic Christians removed the following: Tobit, Judith, Maccabees 1 and 2, Wisdom, Sirach, and Baruch.

The Bible is the most influential book in history. Certainly, the Old Testament has special value for those of Jewish belief, and both the Old and New Testaments have special significance to those of Christian belief. But even outside of the religious significance it is impossible to ignore the relevance and influence the Bible has had on human history.

MEDITATION

How well do I know the Bible? Is it time this Lent to start reading Scripture a little each day?

PRAYER

Your word, O God, is spirit and life. Through the words of Scripture, you reveal your plan for humankind and your everlasting love for us. Help us to make the Bible an integral part of our lives and to prayerfully reflect on the truth you set before us there.

Monday of the Third Week of Lent

2 KINGS 5:1–15A; LUKE 4:24–30

THE RICH CATHOLIC TRADITION
· ·

Truly I tell you no prophet is accepted

in the prophet's hometown.

(Luke 4:24)

· ·

REFLECTION

At one time or another, most Catholics have been cornered by an overzealous non-Catholic Christian in the workplace or supermarket. They immediately start quoting Scripture, and oftentimes their well-argued ideas leave their Catholic targets tired, confused, filled with doubts, and feeling spiritually inadequate.

Chances are, if the conversation proceeds to any length, they will approach the idea that the Bible is the one and only source of inspiration, direction, and revelation. This differs from what we believe as

Catholics: that both the "Sacred Scriptures and sacred tradition form one sacred deposit of the word of God" (*Dei Verbum*). God reveals himself in nature, he reveals himself in the Scriptures, and he reveals himself in the life of the Church.

It is this dynamic interaction between the Scriptures and tradition that keeps the Word alive. If you separate the Scriptures from the living, breathing institution they were entrusted to, they lose their life. This is a major point of contention between Catholics and other non-Catholic Christians.

It is important to note that for more than fifteen hundred years all Christians were Catholic, and they all accepted as part of the Bible all of the books currently in the Catholic canon. It is also interesting to note that the great majority of non-Catholic Christians have no idea that there are books missing from their Bible.

Many modern Christians make it sound like it is impossible to receive salvation without a Bible. If that were the case, what happened to the people who lived before the Bible was printed? What happened to the people who lived before it was even written in its present form? How were men and women introduced to Jesus before the sixteenth century? How were the people of foreign lands inspired to live the Christian life before the Bible was available in mass production?

It is here, in the gap of most Protestants' understanding of Christian history, that you find the beauty of Catholicism.

MEDITATION

What is my understanding of the role of Scripture and tradition in revealing the word of God to Catholics? How has Scripture enriched my faith?

PRAYER

Your word and sacred traditions, O God, fill my soul. Thank you for revealing yourself to me in your creation, in the Scriptures, and in the life of the Church. Through these holy and wonderful gifts, I pray to know you and love you—and my Catholic faith. Amen.

OF PROPHETS AND KINGS

. . . .

Then Peter came and said to him, "Lord, if another member of the church sins against me, how often should I forgive? As many as seven times?" Jesus said to him, "Not seven times, but, I tell you, seventy-seven times."

(Matthew 18:21–22)

. . . .

REFLECTION

The Bible wasn't written all at once, nor was it all written by one person. In fact, a thousand years elapsed between the writing of the book of Genesis and the writing of the book of Revelation. If you had lived in the court of King David (1000–962 BC), the only parts of what is today the Bible that you would have read are some of the stories from Genesis, the stories of the Exodus, the journey from Egypt to the Holy Land, and the stories that we find in the book of Judges of the Israelites settling in the Holy Land.

The Old Testament was written and compiled between the twelfth century and the second century BC. It is made up of forty-six books, and is divided into three categories: the Pentateuch, the Prophets, and the Writings. The Pentateuch, which is also known as the Law, the Torah, or the Five Books of Moses, consists of the first five books of the Old Testament: Genesis, Exodus, Leviticus, Numbers, and Deuteronomy. This was the embryo of the Bible. The section known as the Prophets includes all the major and minor prophets of the Old Testament. And finally, the Writings section includes the historical documents.

The New Testament was written between AD 45 and AD 150 and includes twenty-seven books. It is made up of four narratives of the life, death, and resurrection of Jesus: the Gospels, a narrative of the apostles' ministries in the early Church; Acts of the Apostles; the epistles, twenty-one early letters consisting of Christian counsel, instruction, and encouragement; and Revelation, a book of prophecy.

It is perhaps needless to say that the Bible was not originally written in English (though the way some people represent it you might sometimes wonder). The prominent original language of the Old Testament is Hebrew; Greek is the language of the New Testament. What we have today is a translation into English from the original languages of the prophets, apostles, and evangelists.

MEDITATION

How was the Bible presented to me in my childhood and youth? Was reading Scripture a part of my family? My schooling?

PRAYER

Your word, O God, is rich and diverse. Through many people, ages, languages, and styles, you have revealed your word and truth to the world. Thank you for the variety of ways we can experience your grace and mercy. Amen.

Wednesday of the Third Week of Lent

DEUTERONOMY 4:1, 5–9; MATTHEW 5:17–19

ALL IN THEIR OWN TONGUE

· ·

For what other great nation has a god so near to it as the LORD our God is whenever we call to him? And what other great nation has statutes and ordinances as just as this entire law that I am setting before you today? (Deuteronomy 4:7–8)

· ·

REFLECTION

The Bible is the most profound and sublime collection of writings in human history. It therefore goes without saying that these writings are difficult to understand. Individual interpretation of the Bible is a very slippery path that leads people to great confusion, heartache, and distress. The history of Christianity in the past five hundred years is proof enough of this point. This type of approach doesn't promote unity, and it always leads to division among Christians.

This is why the Catholic Church has, in her wisdom, so vigorously defended her sole right to interpret the meaning of the Scriptures throughout history. The living voice of the Catholic Church stands as a beacon for all men and women of goodwill and announces the life and teachings of Jesus Christ, with tradition in one hand and the Scriptures in the other.

Ultimately, interpreting the Scriptures comes down to a question of authority. It perhaps is no surprise that the greatest obstacle to Christian unity is also the question of authority. The greatest challenge that faces us, as Christians, in our quest for unity is to free so many from the blind subservience to a book and deliver them to a loving obedience to God alive and present in the one, holy, catholic, and apostolic Church.

Throughout human history, every civilization has reached out to God. Different societies have reached out to God in different ways, and many of them seem strange to us today, but they all point to a single truth: Deep in the heart of every person, there is a desire to know God and a yearning to draw nearer to him. Similarly, at every moment of human history, God has reached out to us. God desires to be with his people.

MEDITATION

What is my favorite passage in the Bible, and why? Has Scripture helped me through the difficult circumstances of my life? How?

PRAYER

O God of wisdom, thank you for instilling in me the desire to know you and to love you. Thank you for reaching out to me through the Scripture and tradition to show me how you also want to know me. Amen.

Thursday of the Third Week of Lent

JEREMIAH 7:23–28; LUKE 11:14–23

THE GOSPEL CHALLENGE

Others, to test him, kept demanding from him a sign from heaven.

But he knew what they were thinking and said to them,

"Every kingdom divided against itself becomes a desert,

and house falls on house."

(Luke 11:16–17)

REFLECTION

There are many ways to approach reading the Bible. You could, of course, start at Genesis and read your way through to Revelation; millions of people do this every year. The problem with this approach is that the biblical books are not placed in chronological order, and so the bigger picture can be lost.

A more appealing way to start might be with the Gospels—Matthew, Mark, Luke, and John. Don't just read them once. Read them over and over, fifteen or twenty minutes a day, for a whole year. Allow the life and teachings of Jesus Christ to sink their roots deep into your heart, mind, soul, and life.

The teachings of Jesus Christ were radical two thousand years ago, and they are just as radical today. If you doubt that, consider Matthew 5:44: "Love your enemies and pray for those who persecute you." Before this, what had been the teaching? An "eye for an eye, tooth for a tooth" (Exodus 21:24).

Unless we are willing to constantly examine the way we live, love, work, think, and speak under the piercing light of the Gospels, we will almost certainly find ourselves gradually adopting a gospel of convenience. A gospel of convenience consists of taking what we find easy and comfortable from the teachings of Jesus and ignoring the rest.

For example, let us consider the teaching "Love your enemies and pray for those who persecute you." Since September 11, 2001, have you heard a single prayer in any of our churches for Osama bin Laden or for al Qaeda or for terrorists? Not only that, if your priest stood up at the beginning of Mass next Sunday and announced that he was offering Mass for Osama bin Laden, what sort of reaction do you think he would get?

The teachings of Jesus are as radical today as they were when they were first announced. They call us to a way of life that is both more challenging and more rewarding.

MEDITATION

Who is my enemy? Can anything change in how I view him or her in light of Jesus' command to love my enemy?

PRAYER

Radical and merciful God, through your Son, the Word Made Flesh, you have told us what we must do in order to live a good life so that we may spend eternity with you in Heaven. Give me the strength and the courage to do as you say and to love my enemies and pray for those who persecute me. Amen.

STORIES OF AND FOR ALL

. . . .

Jesus answered, "The first is, 'Hear, O Israel: the Lord our God, the Lord is one; you shall love the Lord your God with all your heart, and with all your soul, and with all your mind, and with all your strength.' The second is this, 'You shall love your neighbor as yourself.' There is no other commandment greater than these."

(Mark 12:29–31)

. . . .

REFLECTION

The stories that fill the Bible are the stories of hundreds of men and women and their struggles to walk with God, to make the journey of the soul, to surrender and allow God to save them. These are the stories of men and women who have tried and succeeded, or struggled and failed, in their quest to become the-best-version-of-themselves.

In some of these characters we find great success in this journey. In others we find great failure. But in most we find an intriguing mixture of both failure and success, the humanity that resonates with us deeply because it reminds us of our own struggles. Most draw near to God only to abandon his ways; then from the anguish of the brokenness and emptiness of their sin, they once again draw near to God and return to his ways.

There is perhaps no better example than Peter. One of the first to be gathered into Jesus' inner circle, Peter leaves everything behind to follow Jesus. Later, he turns his back on Jesus, denying he even knows him. But after Jesus' resurrection, Peter becomes the unifying voice for the early Church.

Stories have a very powerful impact on our lives. They can transform civilizations. A story can win or lose a war. Stories can conquer the hearts of millions and transform enemies into friends. They can help heal the sick. The proud despise them because they are simple, but stories are one of the most powerful agents in history. They can reform the political or spiritual temperament of an age.

What biblical stories will you allow to direct your life?

MEDITATION

Can I relate to Peter? Have I ever ignored what I knew was the right thing to do because I was afraid what people might think of me?

PRAYER

God of truth and power, guide me to the stories of the Bible that will help me lead a righteous and good life. Point me to the examples of those who have gone before me who have been challenged as I have been and who conquered their weakness and misgivings so that they might follow and become more like you. Amen.

PRAYING WITH THE BIBLE

. . . .

I desire steadfast love and not sacrifice,

the knowledge of God rather than burnt offerings.

(Hosea 6:6)

. . . .

REFLECTION

The Bible is the richest treasury of prayers. Some of the prayers are obvious, like the Psalms, but others are treasures hidden among the stories, waiting to be discovered. Amid the hustle and bustle of a busy day, I like to use what I call the First Christian Prayers to keep me in tune with my spiritual priorities. This is the name I have given to the words people spoke to Christ during his lifetime.

When I sense that God is calling me to something or when I have a decision to make and don't know which option to favor, I pray the words of the blind man: "Lord, open my eyes so that I may see" (Matthew 20:33). During times of doubt, questioning, or confusion, I use the prayer of the father of the possessed boy: "Lord I believe, help my unbelief" (Mark 9:24).

And one of my very favorite prayers is the words of Peter when Jesus asks him three times, "Do you love me?" and Peter replies, "Lord, you know all things, you know that I love you" (John 21:17). Sometimes I use this prayer when I have offended God with my words or actions. At other times I use them when I feel hopeless or inadequate in my attempts to express my love for God.

I pray these simple prayers over and over again throughout the day. They allow me to stay connected to God even among the many activities that can make my days very busy.

The Word of God deserves to be approached with reverence and awe. It is all too easy to think that we know a certain story and to tune out as a result. But to do so would be a mistake. The Word of God is constantly new and fresh, even for those who have spent a lifetime exploring it.

This Lent, pick up the Bible and begin a fabulous new adventure in your spiritual life.

MEDITATION

What have I learned this week about praying with Scripture? How can I make the Bible more fully a part of my spiritual journey?

PRAYER

God of the Living Word, I come to you with reverence and awe. Every time I read what you have revealed to me, I am made new and inspired to be better. Throughout my busy day, be with me and remind me that when I need comfort or solitude or wisdom or guidance, you already have given me all that I need to know through your holy and living word. Amen.

THE FIFTH PILLAR: FASTING

Sunday of the Fourth Week of Lent

YEAR A: 1 SAMUEL 16:1, 6–7, 10–13; EPHESIANS 5:8–14; JOHN 9:1–41

YEAR B: 2 CHRONICLES 36:14–17, 19–23; EPHESIANS 2:4–10; JOHN 3:14–21

YEAR C: JOSHUA 5:9A, 10–12; 2 CORINTHIANS 5:17–21; LUKE 15:1–3, 11–32

YEARNING FOR LOVE

Jesus said, "I came into this world for judgment so that those who do not see may see, and those who do see may become blind."

(John 9:39)

REFLECTION

In a world obsessed with pleasure the fifth pillar may demonstrate the relevance of our spirituality more than any of the other spiritual disciplines. You and I were created to love and be loved, and as such we yearn to love and be loved. As long as men and women have this yearning, the practices and traditions of our faith will be relevant. Let me explain.

It is often said that in our present age there is a poverty of love. Divorce rates are usually cited to support this claim. But I would like to suggest that our culture is experiencing not a poverty of love but rather a poverty of self-possession. Our ability to love is directly linked to the level of self-possession that we have. In order to love, in order to put another before ourselves, we need self-possession. The person who has little self-possession thinks only of himself and constantly places his desires before the needs of others.

The very act of loving is an act of self-donation, of giving ourselves to another. But in order to give ourselves, we must first possess ourselves. It is this self-possession that has been massively diminished by the hedonistic ideas of our culture. Broken relationships, soaring divorce rates, relationships that stay together only for convenience, and dysfunction within even the healthiest relationships are just the symptoms. The disease is our lack of self-possession.

All the spiritual disciplines that make up the incredible landscape of Catholic spirituality are designed in one way or another to restore our lost self-possession so that we can once again love God and neighbor and be loved the way we were created to be loved.

MEDITATION

How do I feel about fasting? What have I fasted from before, and what did I learn from that experience?

PRAYER

Loving God, my heart yearns for you. As we come into these last weeks of Lent, may my resolve strengthen, my stony heart be broken, and my mind become more focused on you. Let me keep the needs of others in front of me and be present to them. Amen.

PRAYER AND FASTING

. . . .

I will rejoice in Jerusalem,

and delight in my people;

no more shall the sound of weeping be heard in it,

or the cry of distress.

(Isaiah 65:19)

. . . .

REFLECTION

As with prayer and almsgiving, Jesus calls us to remember that fasting is a spiritual exercise and as such is primarily an action of the inner life. We do not fast to impress other people. We fast to cultivate the inner life. Fasting should be an occasion of joy, not a cause of sadness. Authentic fasting draws us nearer to God and opens our hearts to receive his many gifts.

Jesus instructed his disciples only once specifically concerning fasting. During the Sermon on the Mount in Matthew's Gospel, Jesus speaks of fasting in the same way he spoke of almsgiving and prayer.

When you fast, do not look gloomy like the hypocrites. They neglect their appearance, so that they may appear to others to be fasting. Amen, I say to you, they have received their reward. But when you fast, anoint your head and wash your face, so that you may not appear to be fasting, except to your Father who is hidden. And your Father who sees what is hidden will reward you. (Matthew 6:16–18)

There is, however, another occasion when Jesus mentions fasting. In Mark's Gospel, we are told of a man who brings his possessed boy to Jesus for healing. When Jesus arrives at this scene, he rebukes the unclean spirit, ordering it to come out of the boy, and the child is cured. The disciples, who themselves had tried to cast out the unclean spirit, were confused about why they were not able to do so. When the crowd had dispersed and they were alone with Jesus, "his disciples asked him privately, 'Why could we not cast it out?' He said to them, 'This kind can come out only through prayer and fasting'" (Mark 9:28–29).

You may believe that people do not suffer from possession by demons in our modern age. Don't be so sure. The demons of our modern age are often subtler than the demons of Jesus' time, but they are there nonetheless.

MEDITATION

What demon in my life needs to be cast out? Can I take time for prayer and fasting this week to help me in my fight?

PRAYER

Loving God, hear my plea, for my heart is in distress. Help me to cast out the demons inside me. Hear my prayers and stay with me while I fast from the things that keep me from being close to you and others. Amen.

TURNING BACK TO GOD

· ·

When Jesus saw him lying there and knew that he had been there a
long time, he said to him, "Do you want to be made well?"

(John 5:5)

· ·

REFLECTION

For the Hebrew people, fasting was infrequent and was usually
employed as a sign of repentance. The Torah requires only one day
of fasting each year: Yom Kippur, the Day of Atonement. Four extra
days of fasting were added to the Jewish tradition much later, to com-
memorate the events leading up to the destruction of Jerusalem.

The Israelites fasted at Samuel's urging, as they put away the false
gods Baal and Ashtoreth and returned to Yahweh (1 Samuel 7:2–6).
The entire Israelite army employed fasting as part of its preparation

for battle (Judges 20:26 and 2 Chronicles 20:3–4). Daniel fasted as he prayed, asking God to grant him the ability to understand the Scriptures (Daniel 9:3). At the urging of Jonah and to save the city of Nineveh, the king proclaimed a fast, calling on the people to abandon wrongdoing and violence (Jonah 3:7–9).

In each of these cases, fasting was used to humbly seek out God's will. Over and over again, the Old Testament makes it abundantly clear that genuine fasting involves turning away from evil and turning back to God. Fasting that involves no such conversion of the heart is useless. Isaiah speaks out against fasting detached from conversion, announcing the worthlessness of fasting in the wrong spirit (Isaiah 58:3–7). The Scriptures continually remind us that external actions are insufficient; they must be joined to some internal conversion of the heart.

Before Jesus began his public life, he was "led by the Spirit into the desert," where he fasted for forty days (Matthew 4:1). Jesus didn't fast in atonement for his sins; he was sinless. He fasted in preparation for his mission. And the fact that Jesus was led by the Spirit out into the desert to fast is perhaps the greatest evidence we have that fasting is not merely a physical practice or another personal accomplishment; rather, it is a spiritual exercise.

MEDITATION

What can I give up today that will help me turn back to God? Can I spend an extra ten minutes in prayer and contemplation as I prepare my heart for conversion?

PRAYER

God of Samuel, Daniel, Jonah, Isaiah, and Matthew, teach me how to cleanse myself and prepare the way of the Lord. Stay with me this Lent and help me to graciously and humbly endure my own fast as Jesus did and all of God's followers before him. Amen.

Wednesday of the Fourth Week of Lent

ISAIAH 49:8–15; JOHN 5:17–30

CHRISTIAN PRACTICE

. . . .

Can a woman forget her nursing child,

or show no compassion for the child of her womb?

Even these may forget,

yet I will not forget you.

(Isaiah 49:15)

. . . .

REFLECTION

While there have been many changes in the practice of fasting over the centuries, the Church's understanding of it has remained consistent. The great thirteenth-century scholar, saint, and doctor of the Church, Thomas Aquinas, wrote of these three values of fasting: for the repression of one's concupiscence (strong desires of the flesh), for the atonement for one's sins, and to better dispose oneself to higher things.

In the modern age, we have seen many changes in the practice of fasting. Before 1917, Catholics were required to fast throughout Lent except on Sundays, taking only one meal per day. We were also expected to abstain from meat, eggs, and dairy products on all pre-scribed fast days as well as every Friday and Saturday. By the early 1950s, fast days for Catholics in the United States consisted of one main meal and two small meatless meals.

In 1966, Pope Paul VI offered some new direction for the practice of fasting in the modern era in his *Apostolic Constitution on Penance*. He not only stressed the value of fasting and other forms of penitence but also reminded Catholics everywhere of the importance the early Christians placed on linking the external act of fasting with inner conversion, prayer, and works of charity. In doing so, Paul VI echoed St. Augustine's idea: "Do you wish your prayer to fly toward God? Give it two wings: fasting and almsgiving."

Here in America, the United States Conference of Catholic Bishops issued a pastoral statement later that same year announcing that "Catholics in the United States are obliged to abstain from the eating of meat on Ash Wednesday and on all Fridays during the season of Lent. They are also obliged to fast on Ash Wednesday and Good Friday." The pastoral statement encouraged the faithful to continue the traditional practice of Friday abstinence and also urged Catholics to perform works of charity in the spirit of penance, including visiting the sick and imprisoned, caring for the indigent, and giving alms to those in need.

MEDITATION

Am I able to connect my outward practices with my efforts toward conversion? Have I been faithful in giving alms to the poor and needy this Lent?

PRAYER

God, of fasting and almsgiving, accept all that I have and all that I am willing to give up in honor of your love. Help me to see better how the acts of giving to others and giving up what I indulge in are directly linked to the conversion of my heart toward you. Amen.

HAPPINESS TAKES DISCIPLINE

. . . .

I have a testimony greater than John's. The works that the Father
has given me to complete, the very works that I am doing, testify
on my behalf that the Father has sent me.

(John 5:36)

. . . .

REFLECTION

If you wish to have a rich and abundant experience of life, you must
allow your soul to soar. But in order to do that, you first need to tame
and train the body. You cannot win this war once a week, once a year,
or even once a day. From moment to moment, our desires need to be
harnessed.

Fasting should be a part of our everyday spirituality. For example,
suppose you have a craving for a Coke but you have cranberry juice

or a glass of water instead. It is the smallest thing. Nobody notices. And yet, by this simple action you say no to the cravings of the body that seek to control you, and you assert the dominance of the soul. The will is strengthened and the soul is a little freer. In that one action you create an ounce of self-possession.

Or, say your soup tastes a little dull. You could add salt and pepper, but you don't. It's a little thing. It's nothing. But if it's done for the right reasons, with the correct inner attitude, it is a spiritual exercise. You say no to the body and assert the dominance of the spirit. The will is strengthened and the soul is a little freer. You create an ounce of self-possession.

Beyond these small moments of fasting, we should each seek more intense encounters with fasting and abstinence if we are serious about the spiritual life—not because it is in the catechism but because it will help us to turn away from sin and turn back to God, which is why it is in the *Catechism.* Fasting helps us to turn our backs on the-lesser-version-of-ourselves and embrace the-best-version-of-ourselves.

The truth is, you cannot be healthy and happy without discipline. In fact, if you want to measure the level of happiness in your life, just measure the level of discipline in your life. You will never have more happiness than you have discipline. The two are directly related to one another.

MEDITATION

Am I a highly disciplined person, very undisciplined, or somewhere in between? How does that affect my happiness?

PRAYER

God of discipline and self-possession, help me to better control my longings and cravings. Help me to see I am in charge of my body, my mind, my spirit, and that through my own free will, and with fasting and discipline, I can a achieve the-best-version-of-myself. Amen.

Friday of the Fourth Week of Lent

WISDOM 2:1A, 12–22; JOHN 7:1–2, 10, 25–30

THERE ARE MANY REASONS TO FAST

Let us lie in wait for the righteous man,

because he is inconvenient to us and opposes our actions;

he reproaches us for sins against the law,

and accuses us of sins against our training.

(Wisdom 2:12)

REFLECTION

You are a delicate composition of body and soul. Fasting is to the body what prayer is to the soul. Indeed, fasting is the prayer of the body, and bodily fasting leads to spiritual feasting.

The reasons for fasting are different from the reasons for dieting. Fasting is by its very nature a statement of humility, while dieting is usually linked to ego, vanity, and pride. Dieting is the secularization of the great spiritual exercise of fasting. But dieting is devoid of the strongest motives and reasons for fasting: repentance, self-denial, humility, self-mastery, and the spiritual power that comes from these dispositions.

It is also important to recognize that not all forms of fasting involve food. You can fast from judging others, criticizing, cursing, or complaining, to name but a few.

Two other powerful forms of fasting are the practice of silence and of stillness. From time to time, fast from noise and movement. Sit perfectly still in silence for twenty minutes. After you have become comfortable in the silence, be still for twenty minutes. Be completely still. It is difficult. Yet I am convinced that silence and stillness are two of the greatest spiritual tools.

Finally, we can practice fasting as a form of penance to express sorrow for our moral failings and to be restored to wholeness. The Church invites us to the spiritual practice of fasting not because she wants us to feel guilty or have a poor self-image but rather so we can be liberated. In the process we are given grace to strive with ever more determination to become the-best-version-of-ourselves.

Fasting is one spiritual practice that can help restore the soul to its intended beauty, reduce our tendency toward those actions that are self-destructive and sinful, and reduce our appetite for sin in the future.

MEDITATION

How comfortable am I with quiet and stillness? Today, can I be quiet and still for at least twenty minutes?

PRAYER

God of silence and stillness, help me to sit quietly and restore my soul to its intended beauty. Clear my mind of self-defeating, vain, and egotistical thoughts, and make me whole, as you created me to be. Amen.

Saturday of the Fourth Week of Lent

JEREMIAH 11:18–20; JOHN 7:40–53

HOLD FAST

. . . .

Surely the Messiah does not come from Galilee, does he?

(John 7:41)

. . . .

REFLECTION

Despite that many modern Catholics have abandoned fasting and penance, the Church continues to affirm the great value of these practices as a means for authentic spiritual growth. Throughout this modern era, popes and bishops have invited Catholics to fast and abstain, to pray and perform charitable works as time-tested ways of turning our attention toward God and the needs of our brothers and sisters.

Yet today, fasting is more popular in secular circles than it is among Catholics. Health enthusiasts turn to periodic fasting for cures to everything from insomnia to cancer. Others are adopting this ancient spiritual practice to "cleanse" the body of impurities such as oxidants and the excess chemicals used to fertilize our foods. Fasting has even found a place in many diet programs as a tool to achieve dramatic weight loss and proper weight maintenance.

I pray that as modern Catholics we can rediscover the value of this ancient spiritual practice—not for God's sake but for our own. I am utterly convinced that if we are to develop the inner freedom to resist the temptations that face us in the modern world, we must learn to assert the dominance of the spirit over the body, of the eternal over the temporal. If the spirit within each of us is to reign, then the body must first be tamed. Prayer won't achieve this, works of charity won't achieve this, and power of the will won't achieve it. This is a task for fasting, abstinence, and other acts of penance.

Fasting is a means but never an end. The purpose of fasting is to assist the soul in turning back to God. The benefits of fasting are innumerable, but all these benefits are secondary to the desire to embrace God more fully in our lives.

Whatever form of fasting you decide to employ in your life, you will have good days and bad days. You will have successes and failures. Stick to it. Don't give up.

MEDITATION

What place will I give fasting in these final weeks of Lent? Is there a special intention I need to pray for this weekend and that I can hold in my heart in a special way during Mass tomorrow?

PRAYER

God of perseverance and strength, I put my faith and trust in you. I know it is difficult to fast, but I will not give up. I will fight the good fight. I will finish the race. I will do all of this in your name. Amen.

SIXTH PILLAR: SPIRITUAL READING

. . . .

Sunday of the Fifth Week of Lent

YEAR A: EZEKIEL 37:12–14; ROMANS 8:8–11; JOHN 11:1–45

YEAR B: JEREMIAH 31:31–34; HEBREWS 5:7–9; JOHN 12:20–33

YEAR C: ISAIAH 43:16–21; PHILIPPIANS 3:8–14; JOHN 8:1–11

BOOKS CAN CHANGE LIVES

. . . .

Jesus said to her, "I am the resurrection and the life. Those who believe in me, even though they die, will live, and everyone who lives and believes in me will never die. Do you believe this?" She said to him, "Yes, Lord, I believe that you are the Messiah, the Son of God, the one coming into the world."

(John 11:25–27)

. . . .

REFLECTION

Spiritual reading is an ancient tradition. It existed in the Church long before we had books to read, when every manuscript had to be copied by hand because the printing press had not yet been invented. In those days, this spiritual tradition was mostly confined to the monasteries, where the monks had access to manuscripts of the Scriptures and other great spiritual writings.

Most people can identify a book that has marked a life-changing period for them. It was probably a book that said just the right thing at just the right time. They may have been just words on a page, but they came to life for you and in you, and because of them you will never again be the same. Books really do change our lives, because what we read today walks and talks with us tomorrow.

Earlier, in our discussion of prayer and contemplation, we spoke of the cause-and-effect relationship between thought and action. Thought determines action, and one of the most powerful influences on thought is the material we choose to read. Reading is to the mind what exercise is to the body and prayer is to the soul.

The goal of spiritual reading is to ignite the soul with a desire to grow in virtue and thus become the-best-version-of-oneself. Like all other spiritual exercises and activities, spiritual reading seeks to encourage us to live a life of holiness.

MEDITATION

Do I already have a practice of spiritual reading? How I can make this more a part of my everyday life?

PRAYER

God of goodness and mercy, during these last weeks of Lent strengthen my willingness to hear your word, and respond to the needs of my brothers and sisters in you. Let me reflect on Scripture in a special way this week, as I prepare to mark the passion and death of Jesus during Holy Week. Amen.

Monday of the Fifth Week of Lent

DANIEL 13:1–9, 15–17, 19–30, 33–62; JOHN 8:1–11 OR,

IN YEAR C, JOHN 8:12–20

FIFTEEN MINUTES A DAY

. . . .

When they kept on questioning him, he straightened up and said
to them, "Let anyone among you who is without sin be the first to
throw a stone at her."

(John 8:7)

. . . .

REFLECTION

When I first began to take the spiritual life seriously, I was very fortunate that my path crossed with that of a very holy priest. He was a man of prayer who was striving to grow in virtue and clearly focused on trying to live a holy life—and he was concerned with my spiritual growth. He would say to me, over and over again, "God is calling you to a life of holiness."

In our conversations about my struggles with prayer, he reminded me that I was called to holiness. When I asked his advice on situations in my personal life, and later in my business or ministry, he always reminded me that our number-one concern must be to honor God's call to holiness in our lives and the lives of the people who cross our paths.

He also used to suggest books for me to read. In each of them, I found worthy guides, spiritual masters, and grace-filled mentors who reinforced this teaching that God calls us all to become the-best-version-of-ourselves. God invites us to holiness.

"Fifteen minutes a day," this old priest would say to me. "It's amazing how powerfully fifteen minutes with the right book can stir your soul." In the morning, in the evening, at lunchtime, whenever you can, find fifteen minutes each day to nourish yourself spiritually and intellectually with a good book. Perhaps it is before you go to work. Maybe it is in bed late at night. Then again, perhaps it is while you are eating your lunch. Find a quiet corner at work or at home and read.

You don't need two hours of reading every day, just fifteen minutes. But do it every day. Embrace spiritual reading as a daily discipline. Make it a part of your lifestyle. Remember, Catholicism is not a set of lifeless rules and regulations; Catholicism is a lifestyle. Read for fifteen minutes every day, and it will become a habit—and our lives change when our habits change.

MEDITATION

Can I carve out fifteen minutes every day for spiritual reading? With what books or other materials would I like to start?

PRAYER

Wise and loving God, thank you for the gift of language—the beauty and bounty of words. Given the right combination and inspiration, words have the power to create real change. Be with me as I choose what to read, so that I can become the-best-version-of-myself. Amen.

Tuesday of the Fifth Week of Lent

NUMBERS 21:4–9; JOHN 8:21–30

DISCOVERING THE LIFE OF JESUS

· ·

Jesus said, "When you have lifted up the Son of Man, then you will realize that I am he, and that I do nothing on my own, but I speak these things as the Father instructed me."

(John 8:28)

· ·

REFLECTION

Jesus lived a life on this earth. He ate, he drank, and he walked down the street. Do you know him as a person? Or is he just a historical figure to you? It is crucial that we move beyond the facade of the story of Jesus Christ. We must delve deep into his life and teachings. We must allow his Spirit to flood the thoughts, words, and actions of our daily lives.

St. Jerome once wrote, "Ignorance of the Scriptures is ignorance of Christ." It's a tragedy of our times that people know more about their favorite music group or sports players than they do about Jesus Christ. Get to know Jesus. Read the Gospels. Never let a day pass without pondering a few of the precious words in those four books. Don't just race through them. Choose a small section and read it slowly. Reflect on the meaning. Then reread it and ponder those words.

Allow the words to penetrate the hardness of your heart. Allow the words of the Gospels to erode your personal prejudices, wash away your narrow-mindedness, and banish your judgmental tendencies. You don't have to read five chapters a day—just a small passage. But allow the life and teachings of Jesus Christ, alive and present in the Gospels, to sink their roots deep into your life.

Imagine yourself there with dusty sandals, on those hot days, edging just to get a little closer to him, the crowd pressing in on every side. Only then will we form an intimate relationship with this man we call Jesus. Only then will we discover that he is God and Savior but also coach, companion, mentor, guide, brother, teacher, healer, and friend.

MEDITATION

What is my image of Jesus Christ? How might that change through reading more deeply about his life in the four Gospels?

PRAYER

God, my One True Coach, Companion, Mentor, Guide, Brother, Teacher, and Friend, allow the words of the Gospels to penetrate the hardness of my heart. Allow these words to erode my personal prejudices, wash away my narrow-mindedness, and banish my judgmental tendencies. Amen.

Wednesday of the Fifth Week of Lent

DANIEL 3:14–20, 91–92, 95; JOHN 8:31–42

SPIRITUAL MODELS AND MENTORS

. . . .

Shadrach, Meshach, and Abednego answered the king,
"O Nebuchadnezzar, we have no need to present a defense to you
in this matter. If our God whom we serve is able to deliver us from
the furnace of blazing fire and out of your hand, O king, let him
deliver us. But if not, be it known to you, O king, that we
will not serve your gods and we will not worship the
golden statue that you have set up."

(Daniel 3:16–18)

. . . .

REFLECTION

Reading Scripture, especially the New Testament and in particular
the four Gospels, obviously holds first place on our spiritual reading
list. It has been my experience that all men and women of goodwill

take delight in the Gospels as they become familiar with them. They are the best education of the life and teachings of Jesus Christ. Nothing ignites the soul to imitate the Divine Master more than an intimate familiarity with the story of his life, work, and teachings.

The Old Testament can also be very valuable as a source of spiritual reading. In books such as Psalms and Proverbs, our hearts are easily stirred to live a better life and to strive for virtue through our relationships with God, neighbor, and self. On the other hand, many of the historical and prophetic books require some rather serious preparation if we are to understand the culture and context in which they were written and their intended message.

Beyond the Scriptures, there are also a great many spiritual writers who can be of assistance to us. These masters and mentors of the spiritual life are always available for consultation. The great masters of spiritual writing are able to set aside the issues of the day and their own personal agendas and place at the center of their writing God's dream for us to grow each day in virtue and holiness. In their writings, you will always hear a call to become a better person. As you read their words, you will constantly feel inspired and challenged to change, grow, and become the-best-version-of-yourself.

They are also very worthy mentors, and if you allow them into your life, they will reveal your defects for you with great discretion and kindness. They point out your weaknesses not to belittle you but so that you might grow and become all you are capable of being. They do this by holding a spiritual mirror before you and calling you to self-examination. They then encourage you to make generous resolutions and lead you into divine cooperation with the Holy Spirit.

MEDITATION

Who might I begin to consider as a spiritual mentor? What books could I read to begin to learn more about him or her?

PRAYER

God of writers and mentors, allow me to learn from those whom you have inspired with your Word. Grant me the humility to accept what they have to say, so that I may be willing to improve myself each day. Amen.

A CATHOLIC TAKE ON THINGS

. . . .

Jesus said to them, "Very truly, I tell you, before Abraham was, I am." So they picked up stones to throw at him, but Jesus hid himself and went out of the temple.

(John 8:58–59)

. . . .

REFLECTION

The classical definition of spiritual reading largely has been confined to Scripture and the spiritual masters. But for the sake of the modern Catholic who finds him- or herself in the midst of the information age, I would like to stretch those boundaries a little while at the same time keeping our sight firmly fixed on the goal of this ancient practice.

I believe there is also a place within the context of spiritual reading for us to study certain issues of importance to our spiritual life. Most former Catholics, nonpracticing Catholics, and many disengaged Catholics are separated from the Church over one issue. It may be a different issue for each person, but there is usually one issue that sparks the separation and leads people to turn their backs on the Church.

For some the issue is contraception, for others it is abortion, and for many modern Catholics it is divorce. I suspect that the great majority of nonpracticing Catholics are not joining us each Sunday because of a very limited number of issues, perhaps five or six at the most. With that in mind, we have a duty to study and know those issues so we can build the necessary bridges of truth and knowledge that will allow them to return to the fullness of our ancient and beautiful faith.

If you want to grow in faith, identify the teaching of the Catholic Church that you find most difficult to understand and accept, then read about it. Study that issue. Get yourself a *Catechism* and read what it says, but then look up the source texts, find other books that explain why the Church teaches what it teaches about that issue, and get to the heart of the matter.

Don't read books by bitter authors who seek to tear the Church down. Read books by men and women of prayer who seek by their writing to reveal the truth and depth of the Church's teachings. If you approach that issue humbly, the wisdom and beauty of Catholicism will be unveiled before your very eyes. The issues are so few; let's begin to study them.

MEDITATION

What current issues do I need to learn more about? What can I do to find out what the Church teaches on that particular subject?

PRAYER

God of understanding and reconciliation, guide me to the texts that will reveal your hopes for humanity. Help to understand better your desire for me to respect your creation and honor your covenants and sacramental commitments. Amen.

START WITH EDUCATING ADULTS

. . . .

O LORD of hosts, you test the righteous,

you see the heart and the mind;

let me see your retribution upon them,

for to you I have committed my cause.

Sing to the LORD;

praise the LORD!

For he has delivered the life of the needy

from the hands of evildoers.

(Jeremiah 20:12–13)

. . . .

REFLECTION

There is a great need in the Church today for adult education. Several generations have now managed to pass through the Catholic education system with little more than an elementary under-standing of Catholicism. Over this time, more and more Catholics have decided not to send their children to Catholic schools or religious education programs. All this is having a devastating effect on future generations.

We could dream up all types of elaborate adult education programs, but my proposal is that we encourage Catholic adults to read good spiritual books. Fifteen minutes a day is as good as any place to start. My proposal will no doubt be overlooked by most, and frowned on by others, because of its sheer simplicity. Nonetheless, let me assure you the simplest solution is usually the best, and hidden in our ancient traditions we will find the solutions to most of our modern problems.

Spiritual reading is a perfect example of an ancient solution to a modern problem. If every Catholic were to read a good Catholic book for fifteen minutes a day, this habit alone could be a game changer for the Church in our times.

What percentage of Catholics do you think have read a Catholic book in the past twelve months? This is a question I have been posing to audiences of late. The consensus seems to be about 1 percent.

Now imagine for a moment what would happen if every Catholic in your parish read a good spiritual book for fifteen minutes a day. How would your parish change? If every Catholic spent fifteen minutes a day, every day, learning about his or her faith, how different would our Church be in a year? Five years? Ten years?

Rome wasn't built in a day. Most great things are achieved little by little.

MEDITATION

How can I help other adults grow in their faith through spiritual reading? What am I willing to do to increase my knowledge of Catholicism and spiritual practice?

PRAYER

God of wisdom, guide me as I expand my knowledge and interest in the Catholic faith and heritage. I long to know you and understand you and to be a defender of my faith to friends, family, and all I meet. Amen.

KEEPING THE NORTH STAR IN SIGHT

. . . .

Thus says the Lord GOD… "I will make a covenant of peace with

them; it shall be an everlasting covenant with them;

and I will bless them and multiply them, and will set

my sanctuary among them for evermore."

(Ezekiel 37:12, 26)

. . . .

REFLECTION

Spiritual reading is a great tool to help us keep the great spiritual North Star in sight. When we view everything in relation to our call to become the-best-version-of-ourselves, everything finds meaning. Even the smallest and most menial tasks take on new life, for we come to understand that every action is a character-building action, for better or for worse.

Direct all your thoughts and actions toward the great spiritual North Star. Find ways of spending time with your friends that help you all become the-best-version-of-yourselves. Similarly, find activities you can do as a family that draw the best out of each of you and challenge you to grow. Read books that make you want to become a better person, books that show you how to become the-best-version-of-yourself.

We have become too comfortable with the modern secular culture, and this comfort has resulted in a dangerous complacency toward the life-giving words of the gospel. Too often, we listen to these words but do not allow them to penetrate our hearts and transform our lives.

Cast off the whimsical modern reading materials. What is in those magazines that will help you live a richer, fuller life? When was the last time you read a newspaper and said to yourself, "I'm a better person for having read that newspaper?" We have bought into the modern myth that we have to be up on everyone else's business.

Books change our lives. If you really want your life to change, read some good spiritual books. If you approach these books with a spirit of faith, a desire to grow in holiness, and a sincere intention to practice what you read, spiritual reading will become a powerful tool in your life.

MEDITATION

What do I most enjoy reading? Books? Newspapers? Magazines? The Internet? Or do I prefer not to read at all? How can this change to help me become the-best-version-of-myself?

PRAYER

Timeless and ever present God, I am ready to be changed—back from the modern secular culture, back from my trivial ways and interests. I am ready to learn how to grow in holiness, hope, and faith and live with intention, sincerity, and purpose. Amen.

SEVENTH PILLAR: THE ROSARY

. . . .

Holy Week

Palm Sunday of the Lord's Passion

YEAR A: MATTHEW 21:1–11; ISAIAH 50:4–7; PHILIPPIANS 2:6–11;

MATTHEW 26:14—27:66

YEAR B: MARK 11:1–10 OR JOHN 16; ISAIAH 50:4–7; PHILIPPIANS 2:6–11;

MARK 14:1—15:47

YEAR C: LUKE 19:28–40; ISAIAH 50:4–7; PHILIPPIANS 2:6–11; LUKE 22:14—23:56

WHY HAVE SO MANY ABANDONED
THE ROSARY?

. . . .

The crowds that went ahead of him and that followed were

shouting,

"Hosanna to the Son of David!

Blessed is the one who comes in the name of the Lord!

Hosanna in the highest heaven!"

(Matthew 21:9)

. . . .

REFLECTION

Why have so many Catholics abandoned the rosary as a form of prayer? One reason, no doubt, is the overemphasis some people have placed on the role of Mary and the rosary. But I very much doubt this is the whole reason why Catholics en masse have stopped praying the rosary and teaching their children to pray the rosary in their homes and schools. The solution to the distortion or overemphasis of a good is never to abolish the good in question.

I suspect one of the reasons the rosary has become so unpopular during this modern era is because it is stereotypically considered the prayer of an overly pious old woman with little education and too much time on her hands. In a world where we bow to knowledge and academic degrees, piety is considered to border on superstition. But in truth, piety is reverence for God and devotion to God. Isn't part of the goal of every Christian life to devote oneself to God?

Catholics have abandoned the rosary today because we have been seduced by complexity. We give our allegiance and respect to complexity, but simplicity is the key to perfection. Peace in our hearts is born from simplicity in our lives. All the great leaders throughout history have agreed that usually the simplest solution is the best solution. The genius of God is simplicity. If you wish to tap into the wonder and glory of God, apply simplicity to your life and to your prayer.

Our lives are suffering under the intolerable weight of ever increasing complexities. We complicate everything. And as this diseased fascination with complexity has swept across modern culture, it has also affected the way we approach prayer. Subsequently, as modern Catholics, we have deemed the rosary worthless. But there is real power in simplicity.

The rosary is not a prayer just for gray-headed old ladies with too much time on their hands. It is a rich practice of prayer that we can all benefit from.

MEDITATION

What is my attitude toward the rosary? Can I consider making it a part of my prayer life?

PRAYER

Holy Mary, Mother of God, you willingly accepted God's will for you and bore a son, Jesus, savior of us all. During this coming week, we will remember his passion and death, the suffering he endured for us. Let us join with your sorrow at the injustices inflicted on your son. Amen.

Pray the third joyful mystery: the birth of Jesus. (For each mystery of the rosary pray one Our Father, ten Hail Marys, and one Glory Be.)

Monday of Holy Week

ISAIAH 42:1–7; JOHN 12:1–11

A FEMININE ROLE MODEL

. . . .

Mary took a pound of costly perfume made of pure nard, anointed Jesus' feet, and wiped them with her hair. The house was filled with the fragrance of the perfume.

(John 12:3)

. . . .

REFLECTION

Mary is the most famous woman in history. She leads all prominent women who have earned their fame by living a life of virtue. She has inspired more art and music than any other woman in history, and even in the modern age she fascinates the imaginations of men and women of all faiths. In our own age, Mary has appeared on the cover of *Time* magazine more often than any other person.

I suspect that if we are to reconcile the great disharmony that exists between the role of men and the role of women in modern society we will need the insight of this great feminine role model. Is it possible for us to understand the dignity, value, mystery, and wonder of women without first understanding this woman?

But beyond her fame and her historical importance is her centrality to Christian life. The first Christians gathered around her for comfort and guidance, yet some modern Catholics treat her like she has some contagious disease. One of the great challenges that we face as modern Catholics is to find a genuine place for Mary in our spirituality.

When my wife gave birth to our first child, a son, becoming a father filled me with new spiritual insights. Through my son I have experienced the love of God in a whole new way. But no matter how much I love my son, my wife will always have a unique perspective on his life. It doesn't mean that she loves him more or that I love him less. It just means that a mother sees her child's life in a way that nobody else can.

Nobody sees the life of a child the way the child's mother does—not even the father. This is Mary's perspective on Jesus' life. It seems to me that every genuine Christian, not just Catholics, should be interested in that perspective. In the rosary we ponder the life of Jesus through the eyes of his mother. This can be an incredibly powerful experience if we enter into it fully.

MEDITATION

What is my relationship with Mary? How did my relationship with my own mother affect my understanding of Mary?

PRAYER

Holy Mary, Mother of God, through you I hope to know and love your son. Pray for me, a sinner, now and at the hour of my death. Amen.

Pray the first sorrowful mystery: the agony in the garden.

WE PRAY TO MARY AND THE SAINTS

. . . .

He says, "It is too light a thing that you should be my servant

to raise up the tribes of Jacob

and to restore the survivors of Israel;

I will give you as a light to the nations,

that my salvation may reach to the end of the earth."

(Isaiah 49:6)

. . . .

REFLECTION

I suspect the real reason modern Catholics don't have a more passionate relationship with the rosary is because, in general, we are comfortable with the role Mary plays in our spirituality. For hundreds of years, our non-Catholic Christian brothers and sisters have been accusing us of worshipping Mary and the saints, and I don't think we have done a good job of settling this question.

Do Catholics worship Mary and the saints? No. We pray to them but not to worship them, and not in the same way we pray to God. Think of it this way: If you got sick and asked me to pray for you, I would. This does not make me uniquely Catholic, or even uniquely Christian. There are many non-Christians who believe in the power of prayer. If I ask my non-Catholic Christian friends whether they pray for their spouse or their children, they will say yes. If I ask them to pray for me, they will say yes.

This is the same principle. We believe that Mary and the saints are dead to this world, but we also believe they live on in the next world. And we believe that their prayers are just as powerful—even more powerful. We are essentially saying to them, "We have problems down here. You know what it is like because you have been here; pray for us!"

Our non-Catholic Christian friends don't believe people can still pray in the afterlife. We do. Our spiritual universe is just bigger. In fact, one of the most incredible things about our Catholic faith is the vastness of our spiritual universe.

MEDITATION

How comfortable am I with praying to Mary and the saints? Is there a particular saint to whom I have a special devotion?

PRAYER

Holy Mary, full of grace, thank you and the communion of saints, who pray with me and for me. To you I send up my cries, to you I sing my hopes for myself and the world, with you I pray now and forever. Amen.

Pray the second sorrowful mystery: the scourging at the pillar.

Wednesday of Holy Week

Isaiah 50:4–9a; Matthew 26:14–25

HOW TO PRAY THE ROSARY

. . . .

Jesus said, "The Son of Man goes as it is written of him, but woe to that one by whom the Son of Man is betrayed! It would have been better for that one not to have been born."

(Matthew 14:24)

. . . .

REFLECTION

There are many different practical approaches to the rosary. The first is to focus on the words, which are deeply rooted in the Scriptures and Christian tradition. The words of the prayers used with the rosary—the Our Father, Hail Mary, Glory Be, and Sign of the Cross— are powerful and filled with meaning, but so are the mysteries that we use as a backdrop to each decade.

Many people try to pray the words and meditate on the mysteries at the same time. Impossible! We must decide between the two. On those occasions when you choose to meditate on the mysteries, allow the words to float by. Get lost in the scene. Imagine yourself there. When you choose to focus on the words, it may help to meditate on the mystery for a few moments before each decade.

I also find it very fruitful to identify an intention with each decade. Offering each decade for a person or a situation helps us stay focused and gives us the opportunity to pray for people in our lives.

I don't think we need to enter the debate of whether or not every Catholic should pray the rosary every day. I do, however, think that all Catholics should be able to bring forth the rosary from their spiritual storehouse from time to time as the Spirit prompts them.

Our prayer lives should be dynamic, like love. Our love should be constant, but it may express itself in many different ways at different times. So it is with prayer. Learn to allow the Spirit to guide you to the type of prayer that will most benefit you on a particular day—not the type of prayer you "feel like" doing but the type of prayer that will most benefit you on that day, depending on the disposition of your soul.

MEDITATION

How can I make the rosary more a part of my life? Is there someone in my home or parish with whom I can pray the rosary, perhaps once a week?

PRAYER

Hail, Holy Queen of mercy and of love, with you I suffer the loss of your son. With me you suffer too—for my losses, my iniquities, my weaknesses, and my longings. Thank you for always being by my side. Amen.

Pray the third sorrowful mystery: the crowning of thorns.

EXODUS 12:1–8, 11–14; 1 CORINTHIANS 11:23–26; JOHN 13:1–15

THE CHURCH WILL CHANGE

· ·

Peter said to him, "You will never wash my feet." Jesus answered, "Unless I wash you, you have no share with me." Simon Peter said to him, "Lord, not my feet only but also my hands and my head!"

(John 13:8–9)

· ·

REFLECTION

The circumstances of this moment in history have conspired to present this question to the Church: Change or more of the same? What the Church most certainly does not need is change for the sake of change. And we do not need change that is driven by philosophies such as individualism, hedonism, minimalism, relativism, and materialism. We are where we are today because we have allowed these self-centered philosophies of compromise to direct change in society, the Church, and our lives over the past several decades.

Some believe the answer is to go back to the 1950s model of the Church. Others would like to drag us all the way back to the Middle Ages. I promise you, the answer is never to go back. Throughout salvation history, God himself teaches us this lesson. Adam and Eve were blessed to experience Eden but were banished from the garden after they disobeyed the guidelines God had given them. In the fullness of time, God sent his only Son to redeem us. After this reconciliation, God didn't send us all back to the Garden of Eden. No, he imagined something new and greater. God never goes back; he always moves forward. God always wants our future to be bigger than our past.

There is no question that we will need to draw on the wisdom of the past in moving forward, but drawing from the past is not the same as going backward. The answer is never to go back; the answer is always to move forward. What new place is God calling the Church to now?

MEDITATION

What are my thoughts about change in the Church? Do I think things should stay the same? Go back to another time? Or move forward?

PRAYER

Jesus, in these last few days leading up to Easter, as I recall your passion and death, let me remember that, above all, I am called to feed your sheep. You have given me a model of how to live; may I strive to be all that you created me for, spreading the love of God and the truth of our Catholic faith wherever I am able. You are the way, the truth, and the life. Amen.

Pray the fourth sorrowful mystery: the carrying of the cross.

ISAIAH 52:13—53:12; HEBREWS 4:14–16, 5:7–9; JOHN 18:1—19:42

TO CHANGE THE CHURCH, FIRST CHANGE OURSELVES

. . . .

All we like sheep have gone astray;

we have all turned to our own way,

and the LORD has laid on him the iniquity of us all.

He was oppressed, and he was afflicted,

yet he did not open his mouth;

like a lamb that is led to the slaughter,

and like a sheep that before its shearers is silent,

so he did not open his mouth.

(Isaiah 53:6–7)

. . . .

REFLECTION

Are we willing to change? I hope so. Almost every person I speak to about the future of Catholicism says, "The Church really needs to change," or something to that effect. What we perhaps forget in making this statement is that *we* are the Church, and so the real question becomes: Are *you* willing to change? Am *I* willing to change?

We call for change, but we forget how difficult it is to change. We call for change but often refuse to get involved. Think about how hard it is for you to change a bad habit, especially one that is deeply ingrained in your personality and lifestyle. Pick just one of your bad habits and try to replace it with a good habit. How long does it take? How many times do you fail before you finally succeed?

It is the same for the Church. So I urge you, be patient with the Church, which is two thousand years old and made up of more than 1.1 billion wonderfully flawed human beings like you. Change will come slowly, because the Church will change for the better only as quickly as you and I respond to God's call to grow in virtue and become better-versions-of-ourselves. When you become a-better-version-of-yourself the Church becomes a-better-version-of-itself.

If the Catholic Church is to change, grow, thrive, and fulfill its mission in this modern climate, it will be for one reason: because we become a more spiritual people. Only then will this renewed spiritual health burst forth into authentic action.

MEDITATION

What needs to change in me before I make a difference in the Church today? How willing am I to be an active spokesperson for the Catholic faith?

PRAYER

Jesus, no one knows change better than you. You died on the cross, and three days later you rose from the dead. Forty days later you ascended into heaven and left the world transformed for the rest of time. Help me to transform my soul, to die to sin and death and be reborn in your love and eternal life. Amen.

Pray the fifth sorrowful mystery: the crucifixion.

HAVE COURAGE

. . . .

Do you not know that all of us who have been baptized into Christ
Jesus were baptized into his death? Therefore we have been buried
with him by baptism into death, so that, just as Christ was raised
from the dead by the glory of the Father, so we too might walk in
newness of life. (Romans 6:3–4)

. . . .

REFLECTION

The most dominant emotion in our modern society is fear. We are
afraid of losing the things we have worked hard to buy, afraid of
rejection and failure, afraid of certain types of people, afraid of crit-
icism, of suffering and heartache, of change, afraid to tell people
how we really feel. Fear stops more people from doing something

incredible with their lives than lack of ability, contacts, resources, or any other single variable. Fear paralyzes the human spirit.

Courage is not the absence of fear but the acquired ability to move beyond fear. Each day we must pass through the jungles of doubt and cross the valley of fear, for it is only then that we can live in the high places, on the peaks of courage.

Take a moment to wander through the pages of history—your family's history, your nation's history, human history—and extract from those pages the men and women you most admire. Who would they be without courage? Nothing worthwhile in history is achieved without courage.

And yet, no one is born with courage. It is an acquired virtue. You learn to ride a bicycle by riding a bicycle. You learn to dance by dancing. You learn to play football by playing football. Courage is acquired by practicing courage. And like most qualities of character, courage becomes stronger and more readily accessible when it is practiced every day.

Courage is essential to the human experience. It animates us, brings us to life, and makes everything else possible. And yet, courage is the rarest quality in a human person. The measure of your life will be the measure of your courage.

MEDITATION

In what areas of my life am I paralyzed by fear? How can I become a more courageous person?

PRAYER

Jesus, you are courage incarnate. As you hung on the cross for my sins and the sins of the world, you showed me that all things are possible. You knew that life did not end on the cross. It was only the beginning of a new and glorious eternal life. Amen.

Pray the first glorious mystery: the resurrection

NEW LIFE FOR THE CHURCH AND FOR US

. . . .

We are witnesses to all that he did both in Judea and in Jerusalem. They put him to death by hanging him on a tree; but God raised him on the third day and allowed him to appear, not to all the people but to us who were chosen by God as witnesses, and who ate and drank with him after he rose from the dead.

(Acts 10:39–41)

. . . .

REFLECTION

On the desk in my office I have a Post-it Note that reads simply, "Something wonderful is about to happen!" It has been there for a long time now. I have thought of having these words printed in calligraphy and putting them in a nice frame, but there is something powerful about this simple Post-it Note.

I believe something wonderful is about to happen. I believe it for my life, I believe it for your life, and I believe it for the life of the Church. I pray that you and I will make ourselves radically available to God so that he can use us to make it happen. You see, God doesn't necessarily use the most talented people, he doesn't necessarily use the people in positions of power and authority, and he doesn't necessarily use those who are the best educated.

Very often education, power, authority, and talent can become the prideful impediments that keep us from doing God's work. What type of person does God always use in powerful ways? Who has God always used throughout history to do his work in the world? The people who make themselves available to him.

God uses those who make themselves available. How available are you to God?

It is true that the Church finds herself in the midst of a difficult time in her life. The dilemmas we face as a Church are a cause of sadness for all who love the Church. In mythology, for thousands of years it has been believed that the darkest hour is right before the dawn and that in the hour of greatest darkness the great heroes of the new times are being born.

The darkness that the Church is passing through at the moment will not last. There is a light at the end of it all.

MEDITATION

How can I share the promise and hope of new life in Christ's resurrection with my family, friends, and parish during this Easter season?

PRAYER

Almighty Father, I thank you for the gift of your son, Jesus Christ, who rose from the dead and redeemed humankind. Fill us with the fire of the Holy Spirit, that we may be faithful disciples and enthusiastic witnesses of our Catholic faith. Alleluia, Christ is risen! He is risen, indeed.

NOTES

. . . .

The reflections in this book are drawn from *Rediscover Catholicism: A Spiritual Guide to Living with Passion and Purpose* (Cincinnati: Beacon Publishing, 2011). Minor alterations have been made for the purpose of this edition. The page numbers from which the passages are drawn are listed below.

Ash Wednesday: p. 153.
Thursday after Ash Wednesday: pp. 154–155.
Friday after Ash Wednesday: pp. 163–164.
Saturday after Ash Wednesday: pp. 165–166.
First Week of Lent

Sunday: pp. 173–174. Monday: pp. 177–178; Tuesday: pp. 182, 179; Wednesday: pp. 183–184, 197; Thursday: pp. 188–189, 191; Friday: p. 198; Saturday: p. 199.

Second Week of Lent

Sunday: pp. 205–206; Monday: pp. 207–208; Tuesday: pp. 208–209; Wednesday: pp. 209–210, 214; Thursday: pp. 223–224; Friday: pp. 225–226; Saturday; pp. 227–228.

Third Week of Lent

Sunday: pp. 232–233; Monday, pp. 231–232; Tuesday, pp. 232–233; Wednesday, p. 236; Thursday: p. 238; Friday: p. 241; Saturday: pp. 245–246.

Fourth Week of Lent

Sunday: p. 247; Monday: p. 254; Tuesday: p. 252; Wednesday: pp. 257–258; Thursday: pp. 259–260, 248; Friday: pp. 255–256, 261–262; Saturday: pp. 258–259, 262–263.

Fifth Week of Lent

Sunday: p. 265; Monday: p. 268; Tuesday: p. 266; Wednesday: p. 266; Thursday: p. 267; Friday: p. 269; Saturday: pp. 22, 270.

Holy Week

Palm Sunday of the Lord's Passion; pp. 273–274; Monday: pp. 283; Tuesday: p. 282; Wednesday: pp. 280–281; Holy Thursday: pp. 288–289; Good Friday: pp. 291–292; Holy Saturday: pp. 312–313.

Easter Sunday: p. 323.

APPENDIX

Ten-Year Cycle of Lectionary Readings for the Sundays in Lent

Year A—2013, 2016, 2019, 2022

First Week: Genesis 2:7–9; 3:1–7; Romans 5:12–19; Matthew 4:1–11

Second Week: Genesis 12:1–4; 2 Timothy 1:8–10; Matthew 17:1–9

Third Week: Exodus 17:3–7; Romans 5:1–2, 5–8; John 4:5–42

Fourth Week: 1 Samuel 16:1, 6–7, 10–13; Ephesians 5:8–14; John 9:1–41

Fifth Week: Ezekiel 37:12–14; Romans 8:8–11; John 11:1–45

Holy Week: Matthew 21:1–11; Isaiah 50:4–7; Philippians 2:6–11; Matthew 26:14—27:66

Year B—2014, 2017, 2020

First Week: Genesis 9:8–15; 1 Peter 3:18–22; Mark 1:12–15

Second Week: Genesis 22:1–2, 9, 10–13, 15–18; Romans 8:31–34; Mark 9:2–10

Third Week: Exodus 20:1–17; 1 Corinthians 1:22–25; John 2:13–25

Fourth Week: 2 Chronicles 36:14–17, 19–23; Ephesians 2:4–10; John 3:14–21

Fifth Week: Jeremiah 31:31–34; Hebrews 5:7–9; John 12:20–33

Holy Week: Mark 11:1–10 or John 16; Isaiah 50:4–7; Philippians 2:6-11; Mark 14:1—15:47

Year C—2012, 2015, 2018, 2021

First Week: Deuteronomy 26:4–10; Romans 10:8–13; Luke 4:1–13

Second Week: Genesis 15:5–12, 17–18; Philippians 3:17—4:1; Luke 9:28–36

Third Week: Exodus 3:1–8, 13–15; 1 Corinthians 10:1–6, 10–12; Luke 13:1–9

Fourth Week: Micah 5:9a, 10–12; 2 Corinthians 5:17–21; Luke 15:1–3, 11–32

Fifth Week: Isaiah 43:16–21; Philippians 3:8–14; John 8:1–11

Holy Week: Luke 19:28–40; Isaiah 50:4–7; Philippians 2:6–11; Luke 22:14—23:56

About the Author

Matthew Kelly is a *New York Times* bestselling author of fourteen books, a world-renowned speaker, and a business consultant to more than thirty-five Fortune 500 companies. His titles include *The Rhythm of Life: Living Every Day with Passion and Purpose*; *Building Better Families: A Practical Guide to Raising Amazing Children;* and *Rediscover Catholicism: A Spiritual Guide to Living with Passion and Purpose*. To learn more about his work, visit DynamicCatholic.com.